AF255722

Toward a Postmodern Ethic
of Radical Freedom

Toward a Postmodern Ethic of Radical Freedom

Cornel West and Michel Foucault in Discursive Dialogue

Darrell J. Wesley

CASCADE *Books* · Eugene, Oregon

TOWARD A POSTMODERN ETHIC OF RADICAL FREEDOM
Cornel West and Michel Foucault in Discursive Dialogue

Cascade Books
An Imprint of Wipf and Stock Publishers
199 W. 8th Ave., Suite 3
Eugene, OR 97401

www.wipfandstock.com

PAPERBACK ISBN: 978-1-7252-9415-8
HARDCOVER ISBN: 978-1-7252-9416-5
EBOOK ISBN: 978-1-7252-9417-2

Cataloguing-in-Publication data:

Names: Wesley, Darrell J., author.

Title: Toward a postmodern ethic of radical freedom : Cornel West and Michel Foucault in discursive dialogue / Darrell J. Wesley.

Description: Eugene, OR : Cascade Books, 2023 | Includes bibliographical references.

Identifiers: ISBN 978-1-7252-9415-8 (paperback) | ISBN 978-1-7252-9416-5 (hardcover) | ISBN 978-1-7252-9417-2 (ebook)

Subjects: LCSH: African American philosophy. | West, Cornel—Philosophy. | West, Cornel—Political and social views. | Foucault, Michel, 1926–1984

Classification: B944 .A37 W50 2023 (print) | B944 .A37 (ebook)

09/06/23

Dedicated to
Patricia Ann Wesley, Moma

Carl and Mary Taylor, Parents in Ministry

Contents

Acknowledgments | ix

Introduction | xiii

**Part I: Practical Conditions for the Possibility of
a Postmodern Ethic of Radical Freedom**

  1 Practical Conditions for Theoretical Formation | 3

  2 From Postmodern Prophet to Post-Analytic Philosopher | 9

  3 Existential Crises and Epistemological Freedom:
Cornel West on Knowledge and Truth | 20

  4 Cornel West and Improvisational Metaphysics | 56

**Part II: Discursive Dialogue and a Postmodern
Ethic of Radical Freedom**

  5 Meeting Michel Foucault: Discourse and Discursive Dialogue | 89

  6 Discursive Dialogue on Cornel West's Epistemology | 100

  7 Foucault's Faith: Archaeology, Discourse, and Selfhood | 114

  8 A Postmodern Ethic of Radical Freedom: Radical
Ontology, Radical and Womanist Epistemology | 131

Bibliography | 157

Acknowledgments

THIS BOOK IS THE result of a lifelong interest in notions of truth and reality, and to that extent many people deserve recognition for its conception and completion. And in no order of significance I express my gratitude to the following people and institutions.

First, I want to thank those who had a hand in my early intellectual and spiritual development. To members of the Avondale Church of Christ who showed me unimaginable love during my early developmental years. There are so many to name; some have gone to be with our ancestors, while others are still fighting what they know to be the good fight. And even though we disagree drastically on theological matters, you still hold a place in my heart.

Second, I express my sincere thanks for my spiritual family in ministry, Minister Carl Taylor and Mary Taylor, and to their children who have been like family: Carl Jr., John, Marshall, and Annette. Thank you for your warmth to me as a child and teenager growing up in the church.

Third, I thank members of my family who have shown undying love. On my maternal side, the children of Nina and Ananias Sr.: Aunt Mary, Aunt Dorothy, Uncles Ananias, Will Ray, Benny Carl, Joseph, and Jeffery, and all of my first, second, and third cousins. And on my paternal side, children of Reverend Fred and Mary Joe Wesley: Uncles Philip, Clarence, and Danny, and Aunts Mary Jane Louis and Donna.

Fourth, to my dear sister Detrius, who I affectionately call the embodiment of selflessness. Thank you for your undying love and generosity. And to your son, my beloved nephew Nicholas, stay strong and keep up the good work.

Fifth, I want to thank my parents. To my father, the late Edward Charles Wesley, I thank you for your love and for planting within me the seeds of philosophical questioning. I often think about the many times you would badger me with me questions like, "Darrell, who are you?" and "What is life and the meaning of life?" I am certain that having to wrestle with those questions early in my life followed me even in academic pursuits. And to the love of my life and the most important person in this entire world to me, my mother, Patricia Ann Wesley. There is hardly enough space to express how you are truly the reason for all of the good I have become. Your love is unparalleled and your example of courage and might are the seeds for the budding of any ideas I have.

Sixth, to my mentors and dear friends, I want to say thank you: Léna, Rev. Artis Smith, Rev. Kevin Bedford, Rev. Cole Thomas, Rev. Dr. Jonny Poole, Rev. Dr. George Clifford, Dr. William Bundy, Dr. Victor Wilburn, Dr. Victor Anderson, Bishop Kevin Adams, Dr. Gayani DeSilva, Rev. Dr. Reginald Tarpley, Sedrick Spenser, Dr. Jerry Taylor, Dr. Bennie Harris, Dudley Bynoe, Dr. Linda Bynoe, Dr. Jacqueline Long, Dr. Arthur Murray, Rev. David Isom, Rev. Marshall Sharpe, and Dr. Mauri Jackson. It is your love and many conversations that instill within me the gifts, graces, and affirmation that have made me who I am today as a leader and thinker.

Seventh, to my ecclesiastical leaders of the Christian Methodist Episcopal Church who have invested in my ministry in a myriad of ways. I say thank you first to Bishop Denise Anders-Modest (my mother in ministry). From my ordination in this fine church to this day, you have been a true source of strength. To my presiding prelate, Bishop Charley Hames Jr., thank you for your extraordinary leadership. To my mentor and friend, Bishop Marvin Frank Thomas, who has shown me the quiet patience of humility and strength of fortitude. And to my former bishops who have contributed in your own unique ways: Bishops James B. Walker, Thomas Brown, Henry Williamson, and the late Bobby R. Best.

Eighth, thanks to my academic mentors. First, I thank Dr. Ellen Ott Marshall, my dissertation advisor, who is partly the reason for this book coming into fruition. Thank you for your recommendation (along with Dr. Glenn Johnson) that precipitated the contract for this book. You have never let me down, and I owe a great debt of gratitude for your investment in me. Second, I say thank you to Dr. Glen Johnson. You have been nothing short of amazing. Your recommendations for my admissions into Yale and Claremont are integral for my success and (as with Dr. Marshall) your recommendation to Cascade Books landed me this book deal and opportunity. Third, I thank Dr. Phyllis Jackson, whose courage mirrors that of Socrates. Thank you for instilling within me how to be critical of discourses that preclude well-being. Your work is always on my mind and in my writing.

And finally, I say thank you to Cascade Books for this opportunity to share my ideas with the world. I want to especially thank Matthew Wimer, Charlie Collier, and George Callihan. You have been such an encouragement during this process. Your patience made this difficult and tedious process enjoyable. I can never thank you enough. Also, thank you to my copyeditor, Chelsea Lobey. Your meticulous work certainly improved this final document.

Introduction

This is a book about freedom, which is to say that this book offers a means to transcend political, societal, and existential constraints. We cannot control the conditions of our birth, our station in life, our race, gender, or our economic circumstances. As the philosopher Martin Heidegger contends, we are thrown into our reality. Our status in life is beyond our control, but what I have learned is that under the right conditions and with the right resources, we can transcend our circumstances. I offer this book as one of those resources. As the title states, this book offers a "postmodern ethic of radical freedom," which, in the Aristotelian sense, is a project in character development. What I mean by this is strength of character, which is the wherewithal to courageously transcend constraints, rules, and conventions in order to experience well-being. At the end of the day, we all want to enjoy a fulfilled and flourishing life. For Aristotle that's the telos or goal:

> for both the common run of people and cultivated men call it happiness, and understand by "being happy" the same as "living well" and "doing well." But when it comes to defining what happiness is, they disagree, and the account given by the common run differs from that of the philosopher.[1]

As this statement implies, there are many ways to achieve "well-being" or flourishing. Depending on context or the community, the process and platform differ. Yet a person, community, or context do not acquire well-being at the expense of others. After all, well-being is the highest good. And "the

---

1. Aristotle, *Nicomachean Ethics*, 6.

highest good," according to Aristotle, "is an activity of the soul in conformity with excellence or virtue."[2]

Toward a Postmodern Ethic of Radical Freedom offers the reader a way to transcend constraints, be they social, religious, political, personal, etc. Freedom requires courage to say no to any rule, religious doctrine, or political position "that blocks our blessings" (to use a phrase from my home church). Therefore, transcendence is necessary if one is to acquire freedom, and after years of personal and professional setbacks, this is easier said than done. But with the right practical, theoretical, and intellectual resources anyone can experience radical freedom.

I am aware that this book is not the first to discuss freedom. To be sure, many excellent books on freedom or liberation have domicile in the scholarly domain. Philosophers and theologians grapple with freedom in its myriad of expressions and modalities. For example, the liberation theologies of Gustavo Gutiérrez, Leonardo Boff, James Cone, J. Deotis Roberts, and others occasioned a turning point in classical theological imagination. These theologians presented a much welcomed paradigm shift, reconceptualizing God as an empowering force primarily concerned about the freedom and liberation of oppressed people. Their revisions of biblical narratives to show that moral exemplars like Moses and Jesus are agents of liberation empowered people whom these narratives oppressed. And much thanks to womanist theologians who revised Black liberation theology, given its blindness to the perils of Black womanhood. Sexism, racism, and domestic violence are barriers to liberation and freedom. To this end, the discourse on freedom owes a great debt to the insights of women like Delores Williams, Katie Cannon, Letty Russell, Monica Coleman, and others for their insight and inclusion of Black and Brown women in theological discourse. Even philosophers, like Sartre for instance, writes of freedom and admonishes the bad faith some have at the behest of being true to themselves. For Sartre, freedom is existential. Yet of course, existential freedom is a much easier goal when there are few existential setbacks. All of that is to point out that this book is not unique regarding the subject of freedom. What makes this book unique is the content that characterizes the conditions of freedom.

Toward a Postmodern Ethic of Radical Freedom depends on the following methodology. First, I situate Cornel West primarily in the context of his earlier philosophical and religious writings, because as one interested

2. Aristotle, *Nicomachean Ethics*, 17.

in theory formation, I see West's earlier work as most significant to a constructive philosophical ethic. To this extent, I focus primarily on what I see as West's version of epistemology and metaphysics. I am aware of this liberty given that West never claims (at least in my reading) to do epistemology (theories of truth) or metaphysics (notions of reality), but despite such liberties, an examination of West's earlier work (and arguable some later work as well) concerns truth, knowledge, and reality. Teasing out these two philosophical trajectories has importance to me, not just because they make some profound philosophical point or contribution to academic philosophy (though I believe they do); rather I use West's positions on truth and reality (or what I see as West's positions) to be foundational for a postmodern ethic of radical freedom. Second, I bring Cornel West into a discursive dialogue with Michel Foucault.

Next, this discursive dialogue between West and Foucault involves a method of reconstruction which is, I must admit, a methodology that incurs some risk. My initial subtitle of the doctoral dissertation was, *A Foucualdian Reconstruction of the Epistemology and Metaphysic of Cornel West*. But as an African American scholar, to imply that a white Foucault has something Cornel West conceptually needs vexes my soul. And though I still cautiously employ this methodology, I prefer to call this conversation between these two philosophical geniuses a "discursive dialogue." This reconstruction methodology came to me during my doctoral studies at Claremont Graduate University. One of the most consequential courses I took at Claremont was "Reconstructing Paul Tillich," taught by Claremont's distinguished philosopher of religion Philip Clayton. One objective of the course was to look critically at the work of Tillich by pointing out strengths and weaknesses of Tillichian concepts. The uniqueness of the course (at least the time I took it) was that though we read, assessed, applied, and analyzed Tillich's theology, method of correlation, and existential philosophy, the goal of the course was to tease out of Tillich's writings concepts relevant to our own (the students) social, theological, historical, and cultural context. Then, we had to find strengths and weaknesses of these concepts. The relative strengths and weaknesses of these concepts depend on the extent to which they have usefulness to one's individual or collective narrative. After reading all four volumes of Tillich's *Systematic Theology*, the final paper required that we take aspects of Tillich's work that we found tentatively useful, though by itself incomplete, and bring these aspects, components, etc., into conversation with other (or another) scholar/s. In doing this reconstruction, we created a more viable platform that answers are (as Tillich states in his method of correlation) "implied in human situations."

For example, my final paper looked critically at components of Tillich's Christology, where I lamented the absence of Black suffering in Tillich's notion of nonbeing (among other things). I used components of the work of James Cone, Michael Eric Dyson, and Tupac Shakur to reconstruct Tillich's Christology. Admittedly, I am a bit fuzzy regarding the details of the paper, but it goes without saying that this methodology resonated with me so much that I used it to bring Cornel West and Michel Foucault into conversation. More specifically, I used Foucault's archaeological and genealogical methodologies to reconstruct my conceptions of West's epistemology and metaphysics.

I have divided this book into two parts. I entitled the first part, "Practical Conditions for the Possibility of a Postmodern Ethic of Radical Freedom," and the second part is "Discursive Dialogue and a Postmodern Ethic of Radical Freedom." The first part is a remix of Immanuel Kant's critical question posed in his *Critique of Pure Reason*, which analyzes transcendental and empirical conceptions of reality. The guiding question for Kant in this section of his critique is, "What are the conditions for the possibility of experience?" In his reconstruction of Kant's transcendental dialectic, Foucault raises the same question in *The Order of Things*. And even more interesting, in "A Genealogy of Modern Racism," Cornel West raises the question, "What are the conditions for the possibility of white supremacy?" I simply use the question to state a paradoxical claim, namely, practice informs theory instead of the opposite case. This entails a reversal of conventional theoretical wisdom where we apply praxis only after we establish theory. With this, chapter 1's title is "Practical Conditions for Theoretical Formation," where I discuss my own personal experiences as a pretext for theory formation. Chapter 2, "From Postmodern Prophet to Post-Analytic Philosopher," traces West's thought, beginning with his current posture as postmodern circuit rider back to his earlier post-analytic philosophical work. This chapter not only contextualizes West philosophically, but affirms his scholarly importance and relevance despite contemporary criticisms.

Chapter 3, "Existential Crises and Epistemological Freedom: Cornel West on Knowledge and Truth," discusses Cornel West's theory of truth, looking broadly at his radical historicism and prophetic pragmatism. Specific tenets comprising these two trajectories include but are not limited to denying objective truth, and that our knowledge of the world comes from foundational unchanging truths. Following a fairly exhaustive analysis, I cautiously highlight points of contention with West's radical historicism. This sets the stage for a later chapter where West and Foucault began discursive dialogue.

Chapter 4's title is "Cornel West and Improvisational Metaphysics," where I situate West as a jazzman who zigzags from one source to another to improve realities where vulnerable people suffer. Like chapter 3, this one begins by defining what I mean by metaphysics. After providing this definition, I look at what I consider to be the first ingredient of West's metaphysics: his genealogy of modern racism. I then examine John Dewey's naturalism and Richard Rorty's anti-representationalism and show how these inform the second set of ingredients of West's metaphysics, which are radical democracy and individuality.

Part II, "Discursive Dialogue and a Postmodern Ethic of Radical Freedom," begins the dialogue between Cornel West and Michel Foucault. Therefore, chapter 5 has the title, "Meeting Michel Foucault: Discourse and Discursive Dialogue." In this chapter I begin with discussing my initial interest in Foucault, and then components of his work and theories. Chapter 6 begins constructing a postmodern ethic of radical freedom by reconstructing Cornel West's overall version of truth, with specific attention to radical historicism. Though necessary for an ethic of radical freedom, radical historicism has limitations, which include a version, though thin, of objective truth; radical historicism also fails to incorporate power relations, making it hardly radical, if at all.

I entitle chapter 7, "Foucault's Faith: Archaeology, Discourse, and Selfhood." In this chapter I look at Foucault's example of freedom and then discuss three of his theoretical platforms: archaeology, discourse, and selfhood. I continue with reconstruction and apply Foucault. And finally, I apply Foucault's theories to further construct West's notions of genealogy, individuality, and radical democracy. And finally in chapter 8, "A Postmodern Ethic of Radical Freedom," I introduce radical ontology, radical epistemology, and womanist epistemology. I conclude on a personal note, by looking at my own mother as the embodiment of a postmodern ethic of radical freedom.

Practical Conditions for the Possibility of a Postmodern Ethic of Radical Freedom

Practical Conditions for Theoretical Formation

I AM A THEORIST, but the choice to be a theorist came accidentally. To some extent, through a series of fortuitous events over the course of my life, paradoxically, theory chose me. Now I know that theory chose me at a very early age, but it wasn't until I finished my doctoral work at Claremont Graduate University, and after my first publication, that I realized my preoccupation with notions of truth, tragedy, and transcendence came from the desire to make sense of my life's experiences. And it was actually during the writing of this book, a revision of my doctoral dissertation, that my personal pilgrimage precipitated the theoretical formation of what I propose as "an ethics of radical freedom." This pilgrimage to theory formation, which begins with my early childhood religious experiences, led me to create conceptual mechanisms for transcending tragedy (metaphysical resources) and understanding the dangers of embracing notions of and offering alternatives to notions of objective truth (epistemology).

Transcending tragedy was a notion that I heard articulated (of course not using those terms) from my first two role models: Reverend Fred Wesley, my paternal grandfather, and Queen Esther Johnson (Moma Queen), my maternal great-grandmother. My paternal grandfather was a baptist preacher, and my maternal great-grandmother was a holiness preacher. Their creative modes of expression impacted my existential outlook and instilled in me the courage "to be" whenever faced with inevitable and ongoing threats of nonbeing (to use Paul Tillich's language). I learned through watching and listening to these role models and discovered at an early age the pragmatic value of religious life and language as expressed in African American worship and witness.

Reverend Fred Wesley, a quintessential African American preacher, possessed the gifts and graces of the best of the African American preaching tradition. His seductive oratory and masterful preaching magically infused hope in people who endured the daily and daunting realities peppered by suffering and struggle. Watching him Sunday after Sunday was more exciting than a much-anticipated visit to an amusement park. I studied his preaching like one who studies for an exam that carries the weight of a final grade. I memorized his messages, mastered his mannerisms, and not surprisingly modeled myself after him by pursuing a career in professional ministry. His lack of theological training didn't prevent depth of insight and rhetorical sophistication. The calm that overcame me while listening to him was like anesthetic relief to pain experienced by a youth in an urban ghetto. Reverend Fred Wesley's preaching was my orientation to a world based on feeling without any real appeal to rationality or logic. And amazingly, decades after these early childhood observations, and following years of graduate education in religion and philosophy, I still feel the soothing anesthetic of peace when I hear African American preachers.

My few and limited exposure to Moma Queen's religious expressions are equally impactful. My most vivid memory was at a Saturday night prayer meeting. About ten of us attended and I remember like it was yesterday the magic and charisma she embodied as she spoke. Her expressions were hypnotic and momentarily made us forget about any existential distractions of the world outside. Of course, as a teenager, my worries about the world paled in comparison to these (mostly) African American women who lived with the worries of single motherhood, racism, domestic violence, and economic vulnerability. Later in life, my reading of womanist theologians like Delores Williams, Katie Cannon, and Monica Coleman provided a theoretical platform for understanding how Moma Queen and her compadres conceptualize a God who could make a way out of no way (to use Coleman's title of her dissertation turned book).

Granddaddy's preaching, the best of African American preaching, and Moma Queen's pragmatic emotionalism, defied logical astuteness and intellectual acuity. Unbeknownst to these preachers, they planted the metaphysical seeds that would later bear much fruit for theorizing an ethic of radical freedom. In this sense, for me, theory and practice have a dialectical relationship in the theoretical seeds planted by my grandparents' foundational and practical resources to endure tragedy in its myriad of forms. These forms include anti-Black racism, inadequate education, intellectual inferiority, political disadvantage, and abuse, along with other cultural, social, and political disadvantages.

As a teenager, I dreamed and romanticized about someday being a university professor, which was quite unusual in those days given limited to no exposure to African American professors in my community and neighborhood. However, I underestimated or, quite frankly, was unaware of the discursive conditions that energizes tragic realities, especially for African Americans in poor neighborhoods. Mediocre academic performance and unconscious capitulation of my own inferiority persisted until I reconceptualized a different way to see the world. Part of this reconceptualization required exposure to academic contexts and intellectual resources that addressed the staggering structures perpetuating tragic realties.

My initial graduate studies in analytic philosophy fell tragically short in understanding and addressing tragedy. I clearly see now how my initial graduate education in analytic philosophy was so frustrating and how this particular mode of philosophizing offered (for me) a very technical assessment of reality, the world (or possible worlds), and truth. In fact, most graduate programs (during that time) in American philosophy departments, especially those with analytic leanings, require courses in either propositional or predicate logic or both; which, among many things, provided a pedantic approach to assessing reality and notions of truth rather than engaging in existential inquiry and historicizing and contextualizing notions of truth. Reading books and essays like Bertrand Russell's *Problems of Philosophy*, A. J. Ayer's *Truth and Logic*, Saul Kripke's *Naming and Necessity*, Gottlob Frege's "On Sense and Reference," and Rudolf Carnap's "Empiricism, Semantics, and Ontology," exacerbated my frustration. Thankfully, with later exposure to philosophers like Soren Kierkegaard, Martin Heidegger, and Friedrich Nietzsche, theologians like Friedrich Daniel Ernst Schleiermacher, Paul Tillich, and James Cone, and ethicists like Aristotle, Reinhold Niebuhr, and his brother, H. Richard Niebuhr, I saw value in my experiences of reality.

Alas, my experiences were critical ingredients of my conception of reality (metaphysics). My grandfather and great-grandmother in their own ways taught me that the rational is inextricably tied to the emotional and the relative and subjective ways we see and experience the world. Forcing conceptions of objectivity to a very subjective experience will have a disorienting affect. I didn't learn this lesson until later in my graduate program and after stumbling my way to academic excellence. I had to learn that if notions of what's real don't fit, then don't force them. After much reflection years later, I realized the challenge of trying to force so-called objective notions of selfhood, value, and virtue to my particularized subjective experience (in my case) impacted academic (or limited) excellence. The following examines the early contributor to why I value the discourse on truth and the consequences of this discourse.

Early Notions of Knowledge and Truth: Brother Carl Taylor and Avondale Church of Christ

When I reached my teenage years, my mother resumed her affiliation with the church of her childhood, the Avondale Church of Christ, which, perhaps more than anything, showed me the consequences of truth claims and commitments (epistemology). Arguably, more than anything in my life, my experience of membership at this church set the trajectory for my profession as a Navy chaplain and church pastor. My father in ministry and senior pastor at Avondale Church of Christ was Carl Taylor. Carl Taylor, who lived right down the street from my family, embraced me as a son, and his lovely wife, Mary Taylor, nurtured me in ways only second to my own mother, Patricia Wesley. Their children, Carl Jr., Annette Taylor, John Taylor (currently a Church of Christ preacher), and Marshal Taylor (my best friend during those days) loved me as a member of the family. The love I have for this family and Avondale Church of Christ, respectively, will have an indelible imprint on my heart and soul. In fact, my appreciation for the African American church and community comes directly from this ecclesiastical experience. Unsurprisingly, following in my grandparents' steps and the nurturing of this church, I entered into ministry as a teenager, preaching my first sermon at age eleven. But of intellectual consequence and contributor to my preoccupation with the discourse on truth, was the gifted insight and an oratorical genius of Carl Taylor, who brilliantly articulated the contours of how the Church of Christ generally conceptualized objective truth. Looking back now, I see the impact of religious epistemological wonderings and the seductive ways truth took hold of me and other members of the Church of Christ. The members of the Avondale Church of Christ, convinced that truth, as the Bible, and thereby God's word contend, are both absolute and assessable. Deviation from this truth results in dire and eternally damming consequences. As a boy preacher, I marveled at the convincing and compelling ways Brother Taylor meticulously proved these truth claims week after week. Some of these claims are (and interestingly enough, in most cases still are): the Church of Christ is the only church Scripture authorizes, the Bible and God forbid women to preach or usurp authority over men, instrumental music is disallowed in official worship services, and baptism (the last of a required five-step salvation plan) through immersion is essential for eternal salvation, just to name a few.

To many, these truth claims and convictions perhaps seem trivial and excessive, but to members of the Avondale Church of Christ these biblical notions were absolute, nonnegotiable, acontextual, ahistorical, and failure to acquiesce forfeited ultimate salvation. As a teenager and young adult, I held on to these dogmas for dear life. My close relationship with Carl Taylor afforded me one-on-one tutoring. Consequently, I mastered this legalistic logic by strategically elucidating the apparent proof provided by biblical text. Proving these truth claims was second nature and during my first pastorate at age twenty-one I tripled its membership by espousing what I believed to be irrefutable truths to anyone who listened.

But once I pursued graduate work in philosophy, this pragmatic zeal turned precarious, eventually resulting in a sort of Cartesian exercise in cumulative doubt. Inevitably, I abandoned my parochial post but years subsequent to these childhood and young adults beliefs, I witnessed the psychological damage the game of truth has for some. In this game there are winners and there are losers. Even more consequential was how I witnessed how profound certain notions of objective truth adversely impact well-being for those who lose in the game of objective truth. To be sure, religious beliefs and political positions undergirded by certain truth claims privileges some while others fight for equality, human rights, democracy, and value. Given this ecclesiastical and theological narrative, it was inevitable that I interrogate notions of objective truth in my doctoral dissertation.

Exposure to Cornel West in my graduate studies in philosophy at the University of Tennessee was life-changing. In 1993 Cornel West delivered a lecture at the university, which by itself had a mesmerizing impact. Yet, an introduction made that night by my then good friend Osagyefo Sekou changed the course of my intellectual narrative forever. I was pleasantly surprised when I discovered (that night) he possesses a PhD in philosophy from Princeton and listening to the recorded speech (I personally did) that night over and over, I witnessed how philosophy proper can have relevance to the lives of ordinary people. But it would take another decade before a PhD program (Claremont Graduate University) finally admitted me, and it was at Claremont that I encountered the work and writings of Michel Foucault. To say that Foucault's work was hypnotic is an understatement of inestimable value. His archaeological and genealogical methodologies were music to the ears of a man who often reflects on the damaging impact of subjectivity and pervasive notions of objective truth. Therefore, without any question, whether it cost me my doctorate or not, as I told my mentor at the time, Victor Anderson, I have to bring these two philosophers into a meaningful intellectual conversation. This book is the result of that conversation.

CHAPTER 2

From Postmodern Prophet to Post-Analytic Philosopher

To PRACTITIONERS AND NONACADEMICS, Cornel West has phenom status paralleled to that of professional athletes, and those fortunate enough to hear him in person (especially for the first time) leave inspired, invigorated, and of course immensely impressed. But isn't this reaction expected when one hears a prophet of epic proportions? Celebrity status comes with the territory, and if I may add a colloquial caption, this itinerate intellectual is not without his share of "haters." Lest I get offtrack, my purpose here is to begin where most people know West, namely, as prophetic practitioner. Then I will work my way back to theory, hopefully, to give nontechnical readers a digestible understanding of West. Even then, my plan is to shed light on why his philosophical vision of reality and notions of truth provide foundational ferocity for an ethic of radical freedom. What better way to start this discussion than to adjudicate West from some of the more contemporary critiques, mostly by scholars who claim that West has lost his scholarly edge?

Postmodern Prophet

Perhaps the most relevant case in point is the scathing critique offered by West's protege, the inimitable Michael Eric Dyson, who recently wrote the article "The Ghost of Cornel West: What Happened to America's Most

Exciting Black Scholar?" This article holds back no punches, implying essentially that Cornel West is a "washed up" intellectual who relies on old techniques that lack relevance for cultural and political concerns of our day.[1] One may interpret Dyson's lamentations as proof that West's current work ethic lacks the tenacity that produced work like *Prophesy Deliverance* and *The American Evasion of Philosophy*. What West needs to do, Dyson recommends, is more writing and less talking. The following quotation from the essay gives West a metaphorical "high five" for his gift of egalitarian gab, while reprimanding West for not putting pen to paper:

> West's rhetorical genius is undeniable, but there are limits on what speaking can do for someone trying to wrestle angels or battle demons to the page. This is no biased preference for the written word over the spoken; I am far from a champion of a Eurocentric paradigm of literacy. This is about scholar versus talker. Improvisational speaking bears its wonders: the emergence on the spot of turns of thought and pathways of insight one hadn't planned, and the rapturous discovery, in front of a live audience, of meanings that usually lie buried beneath the rubble of formal restrictions and literary conventions. Yet West's inability to write is hugely confining. For scholars, there is a depth that can only be tapped through the rigorous reworking of the same sentences until the meaning comes clean—or as clean as one can make it.[2]

As a public intellectual himself, Dyson sees the value of the spoken word, and like West, Dyson's appeal to the masses resembles that of his mentor and teacher. Yet here Dyson exalts the written word while implicitly downplaying the power of spoken word. One wonders why Dyson would even risk a perception of disloyalty to a man who is partly the reason Dyson's exalted status and reputation affords him ubiquitous recognition. To be fair, this is a fight that West started when he questioned Dyson's character and integrity after the latter affirmed Barack Obama as a progressive politician. However, publicly discrediting the scholarly acumen of America's most celebrated organic and public intellectual since W. E. B. Du Bois is unnecessary roughness. What appears to be a debilitating jab to West's prophetic expression through public discourse is a blow below the belt. I get it, West's public (and albeit unnecessary) scorn brought out the Detroit in Dyson, but why add fuel to the anti-Black racist fire? Certainly Dyson knows the collateral damage of this insult on West will be a setback of enormous proportions.

1. Dyson, "Ghost of Cornel West."
2. Dyson, "Ghost of Cornel West."

When anti-Black racism pervades academia, and when hiring committees look for the slightest reason to overlook applications from Black PhDs and scholars, to question the aptness of a scholar with a publishing record like West confirms what non-Black people think but refuse to say—at least among Black people anyway—that Black scholarship is pseudo-scholarship, and as one Bible writer queried, "If the righteous one is scarcely saved, where will the ungodly and the sinner appear?" (1 Peter 4:18).

Moving forward, there are two important things to consider about Cornel West without distraction. The first thing to consider is that Cornel West is a philosophical and theoretical maestro whose immortal brand, created early on in his career, will persist even if/when West exits stage. Theoretical trajectories like radical democracy, the tragic-comic, prophetic pragmatism, and cultural politics of difference will have domicile in a variety of academic departments long after the bodies of West and Dyson become "the culinary delight of terrestrial worms" (to use West's own words). Philosophers, ethicists, cultural critics, or religious theorists can never deny the immortal impact and influence of Immanuel Kant's *Critique of Pure Reason*, *Groundwork of the Metaphysics of Morals*, and *Critique of Practical Reason*. Similarly, the Westian spirit will perennially permeate the veins of the academy, sustaining the life of discourse like ethics, cultural studies, African philosophy, African American studies, Black liberation theology, and critical race theory. And like it or not, books like West's *Prophesy Deliverance*, *The American Evasion of Philosophy*, *Keeping Faith*, and *Race Matters* will have tenure and shelf life despite emerging scholarship. Any recent scholarly or nonscholarly work West produces now are gratuitous performances from a composer, who after taking a bow, honors his fans' demand for an encore.

I am the first to admit that recent books by Cornel West lack the potent intellectual venom his earlier work possesses. *Black Prophetic Fire*, *Brother West*, and *Hope on a Tightrope* pale in comparison to the depth and Promethean power of his earlier work. Dyson rightly points out pragmatic differences between the spoken word and the written word. He accentuates West's rhetorical genius and admonishes West for his failure to produce any new serious scholarly work, as if we are only talking about an ivory-tower tenured professor who primarily focuses on the development of like-minded aspirants and regurgitation of new ideas. West has paid his dues to the academy by producing scholars to continue his legacy. Indeed, the academy, and specifically esteemed institutions like Princeton and Vanderbilt, benefit from the presence of brilliant proteges like Victor Anderson, Eddie Glaude, and yes, even Dyson, who, esteemed scholars in their own right, leave their imprints in scholarly areas like social theory, cultural criticism, Black liberation theology, and Christian ethics. These scholars have the academic watch, and the sum total of West's vocation is to ultimately (as Tillich reminds us) provide answers to questions implied in the human situation.[3]

These answers are to questions like social maladies, political disadvantages, anti-Black racism, gender inequality, and heterosexism, just to name a few. West is more a philosopher of religion than a theologian, yet his earlier writings provide theoretical answers. But there comes a time when practice explains theory, and as this postmodern circuit rider makes his rounds, he improves the activity of souls by packaging prophetic theorizing in practical garb. His books provide answers. Radical democracy, the tragic-comic, individualism, radical historicism, anti-foundationalism, and prophetic pragmatism are theoretical provisions from a prophet who has insisted from the beginning of his career that we pay attention foremost to the plight of the least of these. The thread permeating throughout Cornel West's work is his concern for "the least of these." Beginning with his doctoral dissertation at Princeton (later a book) to his more recent publications and speeches, West's creative genius is the catalyst for remedying pervasive oppressive structures and political disadvantages that hinder well-being for the most vulnerable in society. And now more than ever, we need to hear from Cornel West both as a prophet and, working our way back to his earlier development, as a post-analytic philosopher. While his later books and public speeches are expressions accessible to a more popular audience searching for practical panaceas for social maladies, West's earlier writings provide the philosophical soil from which West's practical vision blooms. I move now to the theoretical seeds.

I began this chapter valorizing with the power and purpose of practical expressions showcased in West's later works and speeches, though the vision I present in this book depends predominantly on his earlier philosophical work. Among the many components pertinent to West's

---

3. This phrase derives from Paul Tillich's method of correlation where he asserts that theology "answers questions" that pertain to the human situation. In the introduction to his *Systematic Theology*, Tillich describes his method of correlation: "The following system is an attempt to use the 'method of correlation' as a way of uniting message and situation. It tries to correlate the questions implied in the situation with the answers implied in the message" (*Systematic Theology*, 8).

intellectual narrative, most interesting to me is his PhD studies in analytic philosophy at Princeton. That a young African American male with Black church sensibilities could provide polemical, political, and practical lenses through which he reconceptualizes and ultimately deconstructs analytic philosophy deserves consideration.

For example, his dissertation turned book, *The Ethical Dimensions of Marxist Thought*, deconstructs notions of objective truth particularly championed by philosophic foundationalism. *The Ethical Dimensions of Marxist Thought* exposes the problem of lumping all of humanity into one bowl of rationality without regard for cultural and historical experiences. A more intellectually and philosophically mature West launches from this deconstruction of analytic philosophy's discourses on truth to his more constructive work displayed in his consequential book *The American Evasion of Philosophy*. Other critical texts like *Prophesy Deliverance* and *Keeping Faith* are outcomes of a fecund mind grappling with the disintegration between the pedantic rumination of analytic philosophy and real-life experiences of the "least of these." Later, West rises to fame as a popular and public intellectual with the timely publication of his award-winning book, *Race Matters*. And though Cornel West goes on to produce several more important books and essays, very few of those possess the philosophical rigor and sophistication of the books heretofore noted.

With this, I take a brief look at this post-analytic posture and how this posture precipitates and produces a pragmatic platform where West offers resources I need in my own constructive work presented in this book. To this end, I weave together West's earlier conceptions of truth and reality as building blocks for constructive philosophical and social ethics. Said another way, *Toward a Postmodern Ethic of Radical Freedom* takes what I see as Cornel West's epistemology (understanding of truth and knowledge) and metaphysics (notions of reality) and uses them as foundations for my "postmodern ethic of radical freedom."

Post-Analytic Philosopher

It was the fall of 1995, and I had just moved to my first duty station in Lakehurst, New Jersey as a Navy chaplain, and with lingering ambitions to further my education in philosophy, I set my eye toward philosophy's mecca, Princeton University. The drive there was an experience all by itself. I pushed through the dense and cluttered New Jersey traffic in a hurry to reach Princeton before the academic day ended. My pursuits that day were necessary, seemingly by Divine unction and reminiscent of when a spiritual journey meets destiny. With absolute determination and relative assurance of my success, and despite unnerving and unexpected turnpike tolls, reaching the philosophy department at Princeton University was worth the cost of any and all frustrations. Upon reaching the campus, the hustle and bustle of the fifty-minute trek seemed like entering a different moment in time. What a beautiful place, I thought to myself. Greenery everywhere, European-style architecture as far as I could see, and tall trees standing as guards to protect from any discomfort perpetrated by the sun. After receiving detailed yet ambiguous instructions from a friendly white girl, I eventually arrived at Princeton University's department of philosophy.

I walked down its halls with intentionality, though any passerby could tell you I looked like the proverbial fish out of water. Still, my prerogative had a purpose, and even if I failed to see a single person, the atmosphere, smell of old wood, and the acoustics from the sound of my shoes on Ivy League floors was vicariously invigorating. Though absent-minded at times, my focus knew no distractions. I looked at each office door that showcased names I knew from my contemporary metaphysics, philosophy of language, and logic classes from previous graduate studies. David Lewis, Saul Kripke, and Mark Johnson were the inscriptions posted on each individual door. Then fortune came to me as if the universe compensated my tenuous travels of just two hours earlier. In his office that late afternoon was the esteemed logician, Richard Jeffries. With his office door slightly opened, I knocked on it as if we had a scheduled appointment, and took advantage of this fortuitous opportunity once he answered "come in." Entering his office, it occurred to me that I actually was not prepared to meet someone of his stature, and all I said was "Hello Dr. Jeffries, I just wanted to meet you and say hello. We used your book in our logic class, and it is truly an honor to meet you in person." To my surprise he asked my name and with reciprocating niceties and a charitable response, he responded "nice to meet you too, Darrell." Having enough sense to make this abrupt visit short, I gave my thanks and resumed my self-led tour. And to be honest that encounter was worth the visit. Relishing in the rewards of the day, I figured to try my luck and make my way to the graduate office to see if I could have a word with the departmental secretary. With my recent failure of a master's exam for a philosophy program at a southern school and a meager grade point average of 3.0, I had no visions of grandeur of any possible admission to the top philosophy program in the country. But sometimes pretending pays off and thankfully, the secretary was still around. This sweet and unassuming lady eagerly talked with me for nearly an hour. Perhaps suspicion, and I suspect frustration, may lead my readers to wonder, what's the significance of this trip down memory lane. Without further ado, the following provides the relevant moral of this story.

What commenced as a curious visit to the campus housing the country's top analytic and arguably most rigorous philosophy program culminated in an interview with an administrator who remembered Cornel West's matriculation at Princeton as a graduate student. She enlightened me with firsthand information about a man I could never reach on the phone. She answered every question I had and even volunteered additional insight. She spoke of his prior failed marriages and even provided details about one of them. From there she hinted at his ecocentrism, commenting on the scarf he presumably wears everyday, and transitioned without provocation to talk about West's good and bad experiences as a graduate student at Princeton.

Alas, my purpose for even sharing this experience and story is to provide some sort of rationale and context for the doctoral dissertation West wrote for his philosophy PhD at Princeton, which in my opinion sets the conditions for his career as a scholar in addition to explaining and contextualizing his view of analytic philosophy. Before diving into what I learned that day, I pause to provide a brief discussion of this philosophical school of thought and its relevance for my construction of a postmodern ethic of radical freedom. I fast-forward to Cornel West's first publication following graduate studies, a coedited book with John Rajchman entitled *Post-Analytic Philosophy.*

Analytic philosophy characterizes itself as Anglo-American philosophy and originated in America in the early twentieth century. Skeptical of statements or propositions that lack empirical verification, analytic philosophers prioritized logical analysis, language structure, and empirical verification. To this extent, analytic philosophers envisioned this form of philosophizing to be on par with mathematics, physics, and science, while shunning any kindred connection with disciplines like literature and anthropology. For these philosophers, philosophical problems and questions had little, if any, focus on human suffering, religious phenomena, consciousness, and justice. Instead, they focus on analyzing sentences or propositions, cognitive states of being, and logical exactness.

West and Rajchman argue that philosophy became too professionalized, using science, mathematics, and logic to describe reality. Major philosophy departments eschewed the importance of giants like Soren

Kierkegaard, Friedrich Nietzsche, and John Paul Sartre. More important, attention came to the technical and critical philosophies of René Descartes and Immanuel Kant as launching paths to the logical positivists like A. J. Ayer, Rudolf Carnap, and C. I. Lewis. In the preface to the text, Rajchman notes that under the influence of the thinkers noted above

> by the late 1950s, mainstream American philosophy had become a specialized occupation with precise formal problems, one that eschewed public debate, disclaimed the requirements of literary or historical erudition, dismissed phenomenological and existential thought, and found little scientific and nothing philosophical in their psychoanalysis or Marxism. Philosophy became a recondite recluse.[4]

For example, as noted above, one of the pioneers of analytic philosophy is A. J. Ayer, whose book *Language, Truth, and Logic* dismisses any notion or claim to be true if the language that expresses those claims lacks empirical verification. Therefore, metaphysics, ethics, and nonempirical discourses on truth yielded only sound and fury signifying nothing. Ultimately, logical positivism's endeavors seemed paradoxically too ambitious in accomplishing its own constitutive project, yet the analytic philosophical tradition amassed an appeal and momentum unparalleled by any philosophical pedagogue heretofore known. Even now, the "Philosophical Gourmet Report," an artificial measurement for philosophy departments, ranks analytic departments as the top graduate programs. When West attended Princeton, it was the number one spot. In the 1980s and 1990s, during West's tenure as a student, Princeton was a concierge that welcomed the most elite philosophers of analytic hue.

Returning to my conversation with Princeton's philosophy's departmental secretary, whether he admits it or not, Cornel West was in a quagmire of sorts. How does he credibly represent the tenor and tone of the department that privileges a mode of philosophizing which existentially distances itself from perhaps his personal narrative and definitely his collective narrative? Being the first Black graduate student to navigate through this terrain is enough by itself to place him in the pantheon of great philosophers. Of course, no disrespect to the legacy of Alain Locke, the first Black man to earn a PhD in philosophy, and Joyce Mitchell Cook, first Black woman to receive a PhD in philosophy. And certainly I acknowledge the sizable influence of philosophical phenoms like Lucius Outlaw, Howard

---

4. West and Rajchman, *Post-Analytic Philosophy*, x.

McGrary, K. Anthony Appiah, Bill Lawson, and others. But soon before 1981, an ominous weight was bequeathed to West as Princeton's first Black doctoral philosophy graduate. Will he show off his genius and write a dissertation on topics like linguistic representations, sense and reference, or modal metaphysics, quieting conjectures that Blacks lack the intellectual agility to do Princeton-style philosophy? To be sure, admission to the Princeton philosophy PhD program should negate any suspicion to the contrary. Imagine the professional opportunities assessable if he just compromised his soul for fame and fortune (which West still eventually acquired). Instead he takes serious the lesson of one great social justice advocate who asked (as I summarize Matthew 8:36), "what shall it profit a man or woman if he or she gains the whole world and loses their soul?" As a result, West decides to write a dissertation on arguably one of philosophy's most influential social theorists, Karl Marx. That dissertation, "Ethics, Historicism and the Marxist Tradition," shows, among other things, that truth is fallible, subject to revision, and has a historical and contextual influence (historicism).

Thankfully, the lessons I gained from the departmental secretary regarding my favorite philosopher planted a seed that later bloomed into a polemic against notions of objective truth. Unbeknownst to me then, years later this unofficial interview provided contextualization for what I call in this book "the epistemology of Cornel West."

West coedited *Post-Analytic Philosophy* just one year after completing his doctoral degree at Princeton, and though the book provides a lineup of influential philosophers, the noted influence on West is Richard Rorty. Rorty, who also wrote a book critically analyzing analytic philosophy, is the catalyst for West's notions of truth and reality. Rorty criticizes the professionalization of philosophy departments and laments their estrangement from other disciplines West deems essential for improving well-being. For example, West's most prized prophetic pragmatism relies on a genealogical lineup to include, but not limited to, the religious realism of Reinhold Niebuhr and the transcendentalism of Ralph Waldo Emerson.

The post-analytic posture of West fuels his notion of truth or epistemology where, in addition to the radical historicism and anti-foundationalism of his dissertation (discussed in the next chapter), Rorty's presence at Princeton and mentoring, respectively, endows West with the wherewithal to debunk assumptions that as humans we possess the capacity to asses an objective reality, a philosophical view called realism. In closing, I cannot emphasize enough how this early philosophical posture provides the groundwork for what I see as West's epistemology and metaphysics. But this anti-analytic posture is the beginning of a more robust story, a story that, by the time it's all said and done, will include the vicissitudes of an ensemble of pragmatic sources to include radical democracy, individualism, the tragic-comic, and West's appropriation of Rorty's anti-representationalism (anti-realism). West's radical historicism and anti-foundationalism are critical to theories of objective truth. West's anti-presentationalism and anti-representationalism are critical of theories of reality. Anti-realism essentially critiques the "correspondence theory of truth." This theory of truth argues that there are statements or propositions that correspond to facts in the world, and these facts must go beyond mere ideas and must be empirically verifiable.[5] West eventually wrote a dissertation on the early Karl Marx, focusing on what West calls "radical historicism."

Radical historicism is a polemic against presumptions of objective truth and the grounding of knowledge on epistemic certainty. West's version of radical historicism presents a conception of truth that is both contextual and revisable; it was Rorty's anti-realism in ontology that problematized the presumption made by the correspondence theory of truth; namely, that there are sentences and propositions corresponding with actual objects in the world. And West's dissertation was a critical step toward undermining this theory. Furthermore, other earlier work by West, such as his essay, "A Philosophical View of Easter," also problematizes the correspondence theory of truth. In this essay, West points out that theories about God, self, and the world are not verifiable by some objective criteria. Rather, West argues that theories about God, self, and the world are verified by the beliefs and ideologies of the local contexts where these theories have meaning.

Other articles and essays by West reveal the influences of analytic philosophers like W. V. O. Quine and Wilfrid Sellars. Although the next chapter is an in-depth analysis of these influences, the following gives a brief analysis of how these analytic philosophers influence West's post-analytic philosophy. Like Rorty's anti-representationalism, Quine's "two dogmas of empiricism" serves as the impetus for West's pragmatic conceptions of truth and the grounding of philosophic knowledge. Quine essentially criticizes both the so-called analytic/synthetic distinction and reductionism in philosophy.

Regarding analytic and synthetic judgments, Quine criticized this distinction by putting forth a methodological monism. After Kant,

5. For Rorty's discussions about analytic philosophy, see the following works: Rorty, *Philosophy and the Mirror of Nature*; Rorty, *Consequences of Pragmatism*.

philosophers argued that analytic judgments were true in virtue of their meaning and that synthetic judgments were not. Quine's monism questions this positivist's conception of meaning and truth by arguing that true statements are not necessarily and merely a result of context. Therefore, analytic judgments share a common trait with synthetic judgments; namely, both analytic judgments and synthetic judgments are based on experience.

Quine also criticizes the notion of reductionism, the dogma presuming that isolated sentences within discourse have empirical significance. Quine offers instead an epistemological holism, "which shifted the basic units of empirical significance from isolated sentences to systems of sentences or theories."[6] Beginning with A. J. Ayer, logical positivists dismissed the truth claims of both metaphysical and ethical propositions. A proposition has value or is worthy of analysis if and only if it can be empirically verifiable, and since metaphysical and ethical statements lack this kind of verifiability, they are rendered senseless and absurd. Quine's polemic against this dogma comes from his famous discourse on observation sentences, where he points out that no sentence or proposition may be purely verifiable.

Sellars offers both metaphysical and epistemological positions that critique conceptions philosophers had for years. Sellars' "myth of the given" critiques the Cartesian conjecture that there are indubitable rational foundations in at least three ways. First, Sellars questions the epistemic position that consciousness has foundational beliefs. Second, he questions the position that these are the foundational beliefs from which empirical knowledge emerges. Third, he denies the reality of a transcendental subject who is capable of policing the reliability of knowledge, and that there is such a thing as a transcendental, disembodied self. Sellars offers anti-foundationalism in epistemology, "which undermined attempts to invoke self-justifying, intrinsically credible, theory-neutral, or non-inferential elements in experience which provide foundations for other knowledge-claims and serve as the final terminating points for chains of epistemic justification."[7]

West applies Rorty, Quine, and Sellars in his own epistemological, metaphysical, and existential developments. His subsequent works following his dissertation deny the possibility of philosophic foundations and sees individuals possessing their own uniqueness and capable of carving out meaningful spaces for themselves.

6. West and Rajchman, *Post-Analytic Philosophy*, 260.
7. West and Rajchman, *Post-Analytic Philosophy*, 261.

CHAPTER 3

Existential Crises and Epistemological Freedom

Cornel West on Knowledge and Truth

Some ethical skeptics challenge the notion that there is any knowledge of moral truths that transcend the varied moral outlooks and attitudes of particular cultures. They do so by pointing to what appear to be deep and unresolvable moral disagreements. Moral beliefs about slavery, monogamy, infanticide, and the burial of the dead have varied among cultures. In our own society there are deep disagreements over the permissibility of abortion, the death penalty, and homosexuality. Not only are such disagreements deep and pervasive, but they seem to resist resolution.[1]

—NOAH LEMOS

By pinching him again, for the last time, on the autopsy
table to remake his anatomy.
I say, to remake his anatomy.
Man is sick because he is badly constructed.
We must make up our minds to strip him bare in order to
scrape off the animalcule that itches him mortally,
god,

---

1. Lemos, "Epistemology and Ethics," 479–512.

and god

his organs.

For you can tie me up if you wish,

but there is nothing more useless than an organ.

When you will have made him a body without organs,

then you will have delivered him from all his automatic

reactions and restored him to his true freedom.[2]

—ANTONIN ARTAUD

THE EPIGRAPHS ABOVE, I believe, diagnose the ontological (state of being) conditions of those whose allegiance to a sovereign power (be it God or an Ideal) facilitate a forfeiture of their own freedom. The first epigraph comes from Noah Lemos' article "Epistemology and Ethics," where this epigraph, in part, supports my position that convictions about truth, belief, and knowledge inform moral and ethical commitments. Later I will discuss in more detail how acceptance of absolute moral truths can have ontologically damaging affects. However, Lemos here makes a meta-ethical (justifying a moral position) point, namely, that what one accepts as true, determines the values one embraces. In other words, one's epistemology informs one's ethics. I know that maybe to nonacademics and nonphilosophers the word "epistemology" seems weighty, heavy, and lacking in relevance to every-day lives of ordinary people. Yet the practical level, particularly in context where truth and the acquisition of knowledge carry much weight, one's epistemological commitments can effect the well-being of others. What one thinks about truth or sees as foundational knowledge, determines one's moral commitments and beliefs.

Remember earlier Aristotle's conjecture, "well-being or happiness is the highest good in accordance with virtue."[3] To be sure, well-being is the goal of every person. To ultimately experience well-being, we have to exercise virtue or moral behavior. Similarly, an ethics of radical freedom seeks for a goal of well-being, and this well-being converges with conceptions of truth and beliefs that don't bind one's sense of being but rather build one's sense of being. Belief claims and our view of truth determine how we treat

2. Artaud, *To Have Done*, 570–71.

3. Aristotle, *Nicomachean Ethics*, 6.

people and even how we see ourselves. An ethic of radical freedom eschews any epistemological position that precludes well-being. What's at stake is protracted racism, sexism, heterosexism, mistreatment to undocumented workers, agism, ableism, you name it. In this regard, epistemology matters, and what we accept as truth has the potential to cause existential damage and disadvantage to some by virtue of their race, gender, sexuality, etc.; truth, in this case can preclude well-being.

The second epigraph are verses from Antonin Artaud's *To Have Done with the Judgement of God*, which provides a forensic assessment of how the body and its organs construe a morally conditioned creature. My reason for referring to Artaud has little to do with the point he makes in his play, which provides an argument for atheism. As my narrative heretofore discussed shows, I am no atheist. Rather, I reference this play to show how our subjective conceptions of God may result in objective moral claims.

For example, the truth claims espoused by Carl Taylor and members of the Avondale Church of Christ comprise dogmatic notions that require compliance. Failure to adhere to acceptable notions of truth leads to literal forfeiture of eternal life, or even worse, eternal damnation, even if some of these claims negatively impact their well-being and preclude flourishing. A consequential moral claim is that God forbids women to usurp authority over men, and that God disallows them a right to ordination. In many Churches of Christ, women cannot serve as pastors or engage in any leadership capacity where men are present. Avondale Church of Christ is one example among other religious and political contexts that appeal to absolute truth or truths. What I mean by absolute here is that regardless of any circumstance, whether religious or political, acceptable truth prevails. Truth here not only prevails, but we have access to truth. Even more concerning is that in similar religious contexts, truth claims like this come from God, who is presumably the ultimate source of truth. Appeal to a higher source of truth is near and dear to people's hearts, to the extent that some may even make political, ecclesiastical, and personal decisions against their own interests.

Upon leaving the church of my childhood for more reasons than I can express here, I recall a confrontational conversation with a member of the Church of Christ. As two ships passing in the night, we spoke past each other without any real possibility of a conceptual connection. Regardless of exposing obvious fallacies of truth claims she espoused, her belief system shielded any possibility of consensus. Without a single class in logic or contemporary epistemology, she expressed a tautology with the confidence of a philosophy professor. "Darrell, the truth is the truth," was her reply to what I thought was a compelling argument. Since a tautology is a necessarily true statement, then any belief or absolutely true statement in her canon of beliefs requires her uncompromising allegiance. Some of these beliefs are "women are subservient to men," "God does not allow the ordination of women," and "women are weaker vessels than men." Interestingly, each of these belief statements precludes ethical commitments that limited freedom or well-being.

The above example of my friend is one of many similar scenarios that harm well-being. Even in politics, beliefs and truth claims like natural design for marriage result in passing legislation regarding rights for same-sex marriages. The straightforward rationale is that the God-designed or the natural design for marriage is between a man and woman. And perhaps even more interesting here is that most of the states passing this type of legislation are Bible belt states with politically conservative leanings. For example, there is an incredibly evangelistic influence in states like Arkansas, Georgia, Kentucky, Louisiana, Mississippi, and Tennessee, and not surprisingly, these states promote an outright denial for same-sex marriages. To be clear, my agenda is to show how notions of truth impede well-being. Making a case for same-sex marriages I leave up to other more capable champions of social justice. But an ethics of radical freedom intends to debunk foundational assumptions about humanity that result from subjective conditioning instead of an appeal to an objective truth.

To promote objective and absolute truth downplays the impact culture and history contribute to one's beliefs. When someone advises "be objective," they assume the ability to see or think about a particular thing without any contributing factors. Similarly, "absolute truth" maintains its truth value and status at all times and independent of history and context. Proponents of absolute truth and objectivity, to a large extent, see practical commitments following from foundational beliefs from which other beliefs follow. These foundational beliefs are kindred conceptions of absolute truth and objectivity in that neither require proof. These beliefs are intuitive, and do not need to have some special experience or revelation to know or to access them. Philosophically speaking, these are necessarily true beliefs, and are known as *a priori*. *A priori* knowledge exists "prior" to experience. An example of *a priori* knowledge is the concept of 1 + 1= 2, since this concept is a fact independent of context, history, and culture. No one disputes its objective and absolute status. However, mathematical facts differ from beliefs about race, gender, culture, and sexuality. And propositions like 1 + 1 =2 pose no existential threat to well-being and flourishing, where foundational beliefs like "women are naturally inferior to men," or "the white race is the superior race," or "the natural and Divine design for marriage is heterosexual" impede flourishing.

The official philosophical position promoting *a priori* foundational beliefs is what philosophers baptize as "foundationalism." Practitioners and nonphilosophers who commit to certain dogmatic assertions like the ones about race and gender exclude technical philosophical words like foundationalism, though, unbeknownst, they champion it nonetheless. Earlier anecdotes I provided about my childhood church experiences showcase scenarios where commitments tagged foundational truth preclude well-being and delimit freedom. And like the queried slave scourged by his dungeon, many provide ropes that lynch and destroy their own abundant potential. No worries, however, because an ethic of radical freedom offers an alternative to these foundational beliefs and absolute and objective truth claims.

The philosophical alternative setting the conditions to healthier conceptions of personhood is the epistemology of Cornel West, expressed more broadly in his conception of "radical historicism." A much detailed explanation of this phrase comes later. But lest I turn the reader off, to lighten the pedantic punch of such a highfalutin philosophical phrase (as my Granny would say), perhaps a shorthand definition is in order. In his book *The Ethical Dimensions of Marxist Thought*, "radical historicism" simply situates truth within the context of culture and history. Which is to say, that what we accept as truth today may change depending on its usage during another historical moment. And as unconvincing as this brief depiction is to some, I hope that one may find the later more detailed depiction more convincing. Unpacking "radical historicism," as West sees it, requires further probing into subsidized accompaniments, which are anti-foundationalism and anti-realism. All notions are simply different sides of the same philosophical portrait, painting a picture of the "epistemology of Cornel West." Of course, first things first, and before probing more deeply into West's epistemology or theory of truth, I shall provide a clear and working definition of epistemology. Therefore, immediately below is a succinct working definition of epistemology, at least my usage of it anyhow. Next, given that theoretical formation entails revising or refuting antecedent theories, careful analysis of the philosophical influences on West's epistemology clearly forges pathways to a better understanding of West's own theory. Among these influences, two philosophers directly and distinctly contribute to what I see as the epistemology of Cornel West. In ranking order of significance, the two philosophers are the Richard Rorty and W. V. O. Quine. But first, a definition of my usage of epistemology is in order.

Working Definition of Epistemology

Generally speaking, epistemology articulates theories of knowledge of truth and has roots going as far back (and even further) to the ancient philosopher Plato. Proponents of objective truth owe some credit to Plato, whose epistemology promotes prerequisite knowledge prior to experience. Any ideas we have did not come to us through learning or pedagogy. To the contrary, our souls, which are immortal, housed ideas and knowledge prior to our current earthly sojourn. Our current knowledge of things showcases what we already know rather than something we've learned. In fact, we don't learn anything, according to Plato, we remember. However, some remember better than others, and here is where Plato gives a metaphorical "shout out" to philosophers. This is because philosophers best exemplify knowledge recollection, and given this epistemological advantage, Plato's ideal society is one where philosophers rule and make legislative decisions. Gifted with the propensity to apprehend infallible truths, these philosopher kings/queens, for Plato, are reliable in adjudicating justice, presumably without prejudice and bias. Of course, this is one philosophical position, among others.

Another epistemological ally for proponents of objective reality and absolute truth is Rene Descartes, whose epistemological project begins, pretentiously, by doubting everything his senses apprehend. Since, in one instance I perceive an object as red, and on another occasion I see the same object as yellow, the unreliability of my sense experiences is proven. Questioning the reliability of our senses leads even Descartes to doubt his own existence. This project in methodical doubt culminates with Descartes realizing that doubting entails thinking. If he is thinking, even when doubting, he inevitably exists. This "ah-ha" moment occasions the famous dictum, "I think therefore I am." The fact that thinking necessarily implies existence occasions the first indubitable truth in Descartes' epistemology. This discovery proves the power of innate ideas we intuit without experience. Cartesian epistemology lays the foundation for the mind/body divide, later informing theories like "realism in ontology" and "mental states and intentionality" espoused by some analytic philosophers like Alonzo Church[4] and John Searle.[5]

The opposite side of this epistemological story is the empiricism championed by philosopher John Locke, who contests and critiques the Cartesian confidence in innate ideas. Unlike Descartes' reluctance to trust sensory experience, Locke's epistemology relies entirely on that experience. The mind is an empty slate on which experience writes, opines Locke.[6] The mind's content, similar to a computer, relies on available and accessible input. Continuing Locke's legacy is David Hume's empiricism, which sees sensation and ideas collaboratively rather than dichotomously. For Hume, sensations immediately accessible to the mind create impressions and ideas that are reflections of the initial impression.[7] For example, one's idea of heat comes from an initial sensual experience of touching something hot—like an oven, perhaps. For both Locke and Hume, notions of truth, like acquiring knowledge, do not require an outright rejection of sensation or experience.

Perhaps the superstar of modern epistemology is Immanuel Kant, who contends that knowledge is a correspondence between concepts and perceptions. Kant's monumental *Critique of Pure Reason* is an exhaustive analysis and, at times, polemic against rationalism and empiricism. He argues that there is value in both, without leaning in favor of one over the other. Ideas are concepts of our understanding and sensations provide the data of experience. In other words, both go together. His objective is to critique and analyze reason and not to disregard reality. Like Descartes, for Kant the mind is capable of apprehending absolute truth and he agrees with Locke that some knowledge is only possible with experience. For Kant, one can apprehend moral truths without experience. For example, in his book *Groundwork of the Metaphysics of Morals*, Kant claims that "moral truths" are absolute regardless of the context or historical circumstances.[8]

For analytic philosophy, contemporary epistemology becomes incredibly more technical and relies predominantly on logic and logical analysis. Stated earlier, for instance, the logical positivism of philosophers like A. J. Ayer and Rudolf Carnap (among other philosophers) saw language as a

---

4. See Church, "Intensional Semantics," 77–84.

5. Searle, "Proper Names and Intentionality," 326–42.

6. Nidditch, *John Locke*.

7. Hume, *Enquiry Concerning Human Understanding*.

8. Kant, *Groundwork*, 21–23.

critical resource for depicting and describing reality. Language here must have empirical credibility, in that language can verify the phenomena to which it refers. This means of philosophizing provides the stage wherein enters the cerebral chorus of more contemporary analytic philosophers. Epistemology performed by these analytic voices is a remix of the rationalism, empiricism, and idealism of Descartes, Hume, and Kant. On this stage is where renditions of American Pragmatism and Cornel West, respectively, sing off-key. Rather than espousing traditional epistemology, a new chorus enters the philosophical stage offering an anti-epistemology epistemology.

In his book, *The American Evasion of Philosophy*, Cornel West problematizes "epistemology-centered philosophy," which is not a rejection of epistemology itself, but rather a critique of the Cartesian assertion of indubitable and infallible truths. Even in the book's title, West uses "evasion" as a prophetic polemic to any philosophy and more specifically, epistemology, that ignores social and existential vulnerabilities of ordinary people. *The American Evasion of Philosophy* is, in my humble position, hands down West's most consequential work. Later, I will dive deeper into this important book, but for now, it's best to explore the philosophical climate prior to its publication. What we see now in public spaces and auditoriums packed with crowds is prophetic wisdom from an itinerant sage. But an earlier posture is that of a post-analytic philosopher who wrestled with tenets of his graduate training. Wrestling produced wisdom. But wisdom's arrival is not absent of antecedent influences that help shape and form Cornel West's conceptions about truth and the world. Therefore, it is important to provide space for such an exploration and doing so will better contextualize West's epistemology. This contextualization begins with the influence of Richard Rorty, who injects post-analytic philosophy into the intellectual veins of a young West. Engaging Rorty not only contextualizes West's epistemology, but given Rorty's courageous critique of analytic philosophy, explains West's fixation with courage and Socratic questioning. We now travel down this Rortyean road, the pragmatic path toward the epistemology of Cornel West.

The Rortyean Road to a West's Epistemology

In his memoir, *Brother West: Living and Loving Out Loud* (2009), Cornel West's exposure to Richard Rorty takes place during his graduate work at

Princeton in 1973,[9] and this experience directly impacts West's ideas. Like West, Rorty attended academic institutions heavily influenced by the analytic tradition. But as destiny demands, West's student years at Princeton came at a critical moment for Rorty. Though Rorty's academic narrative culminates with being one of analytic philosophy's most compelling critics, most of his career enjoyed an intellectual romance with this tradition. This romance begins with his undergraduate studies at the University of Chicago, where Rorty worked with noted analytic philosopher and logical positivist, Rudolf Carnap. Following this undergraduate orientation to analytic philosophy, Rorty matriculates for four years as a PhD student at Yale University, eventually writing a dissertation entitled "The Concept of Potentiality." A tailor-made fit for a strong analytic philosophy department, Rorty spends the span of approximately eighteen years at Princeton University. In 1970 this intellectual romance reached a crossroads when Rorty published his groundbreaking essay, "Cartesian Epistemology and Changes in Ontology."

In this essay, Rorty challenges epistemological approaches that affirm our ability to possess knowledge and conceptions of truth independent of ordinary daily experiences.[10] Even the title itself signals the brewing of alternative methods to how philosophers thought about truth and knowledge. In fact, the phrase "Changes in Ontology" in the title alerts readers of Rorty's agenda, namely, asserting the correlation between epistemology and diversity of experiences and modes of being. Since ontology is, by definition, "the study of being," Rorty quiets the roar of the Enlightenment's ferocious claim of ubiquitous rationality, while at the same time exposing the Enlightenment's miscalculations about *being* in general. *Being*, according to the Enlightenment mindset, lumped all of humanity into one basket of existence. Postmodern theorists describe this one basket of existence, a meta-narrative approach to understanding "the nature of being." Rorty contests this way of thinking and proposes, instead, that people change and epochs change. With changes like these come new ways of thinking and new ways of how we see the world. A case in point is Thomas Kuhn's notion of paradigm, signaling a shift from and interrogation of dominate discourses and ways of thinking.[11] Neil Gross points out that, like Kuhn who questions presumptions of objectivity made by science, Rorty suggests that concerns

9. West and Ritz, *Brother West*, 82.

10. Rorty, "Cartesian Epistemology," 273–92.

11. Gross, *Richard Rorty*, 204.

about ontology change as new epochs evolve. Like Kuhn, Rorty suggests that paradigms shift in philosophical discourse and thereby change what kind of questions one may ask. Raising different questions does not imply a flaw or deficiency in prior epochs. Instead, evolving social, political, and cultural apparatuses occasion new sets of queries.[12]

Rorty later includes "Cartesian Epistemology and Changes in Ontology" in *Philosophy and the Mirror of Nature,* to support the argument that philosophers must reconsider alternative ways of addressing philosophical problems. Rorty lays out his thesis for the book in a letter to the president of the Guggenheim Foundation, a foundation that sponsored the book project through a fellowship in 1973.[13]

> The book attempts to present "modern day philosophy" (i.e., epistemology and metaphysics since Descartes) as a working-out of the consequences of Descartes' picture of human knowledge as an ordering of inner representations. I argue that the image of the Mind as a Mirror of Nature brought in its train the notion of the Mind as a metaphysically distinct realm of being, and thus the notion of philosophy as a discipline which centers around the questions "How can the subject get to the object (through the veil of ideas)?" and "How can man be both a Mind—an hardly understood Glassy Essence—and something material?" In other words, I argue that the notion of philosophy as constituted by epistemology and metaphysics is a relatively recent and parochial one—that without problems about the veil of ideas and the relation between mind and body which were barely formulated (and could have been intelligible before Descartes) we have [no] notion of "epistemology" or "metaphysics."[14]

This quotation offers a postmodern conception of truth and knowledge (epistemology) and how we experience the world (metaphysics), one insisting that mind and body cooperate in understanding the world and reality. In other words, the mind does not exist in isolation from the body, which encases it. We have to consider, then, that the body, and therefore the mind, possess a history, culture, and context. The body contributes to the mind's content, that is, what the mind believes and values.

12. Gross, *Richard Rorty,* 204.

13. Gross, *Richard Rorty,* 204.

14. Richard Rorty to Gordon Ray, September 16, 1974, RRP. Although this is a quotation from Rorty's letter to Mr. Ray, this is also quoted in Gross, *Richard Rorty,* 205.

The corporative connection of mind and body differs from how René Descartes thought, and as Rorty correctly sees it, this Cartesian mindset overstates the mind's capacity to obtain knowledge independent of history and culture. This capability ascribes to the mind transcendental power, which points to its power to intuit the existence of transcendental realities, like God, a self, moral truths, etc. For example, in his ontological argument for the existence of God, Descartes says that the fact we have an idea of God, proves that God exists. Even when a person denies God's existence, they still have an idea of God, proving God's existence. An idea that demonstrates that there are innate ideas the mind possesses regardless of the history, context, and culture of the body that houses the mind. This argument for God's existence is just one practical example of just how strong the mind is and what beliefs the mind can access. Stronger minds compel more vulnerable minds of God's truth, which oftentimes is at the chagrin of others. How is this possible? *Transcendental* means *transcending* physical and empirical phenomena, and whatever objects (e.g., God, pastor, politician) enjoying such privilege and power to determine truth, moral rules, and foundational beliefs, which control behavior of those beholden to those contexts.

During this time, Rorty published *Philosophy and the Mirror of Nature* (1978), which lays out Rorty's views about theories of knowledge and truth and in doing so he provides a critical assessment of contemporary discussions on the matter. *Philosophy and the Mirror of Nature* is an exhaustive historical analysis of these theories beginning with Descartes and culminating with more contemporary theories. Rorty disagrees with Cartesian conceptions of infallible rational beliefs, and he also exposes weaknesses in the so-called correspondence theory truth. The latter contends that what's in reality mirrors what's in our minds, and by engaging philosophers like Quine and Sellars, Rorty offers a more pragmatic version of these theories.

Rorty contests the existence of a transcendental object possessing such power by offering an epistemological alternative he calls, "de-transcendentalizing the subject." That is, Rorty questions the possibility of a disembodied mind (or what Descartes calls "cogito") fully capable of apprehending the world without reliance on the senses. Through the influence of Descartes, modern epistemology views the mind as a distinct entity, which is perhaps one reason why analytic philosophers overlooked culture, race, and narrative from their philosophizing. This social and existential absent-mindedness provides the pragmatic entrance of Cornel West on the intellectual scene. West carries on the Rortyan project in his noted philosophical work, though even his less pedantic reflections are residues from earlier rigorous philosophizing. Notions of race, gender, sexuality, progressive politics, blues sensibilities, and the tragic-comic are talking points West highlights in his many public appearances across the country. Yet thanks to the earlier theoretical work contesting the dangers of Cartesian epistemology and subsequent analytic renditions that endorse grounded knowledge, objective truth, and a transcendental mind, West now exhales from his laborious labor a couple of decades earlier. And now that I've stepped onto the epistemological stage on which West enters the conversation about truth and knowledge, I now look more deeply into his labor and work.

Cornel West on Truth and Knowledge

The contentiousness Rorty expressed toward contemporary notions of truth noticeably influences West, whose existential alliance with oppressed people requires a pragmatic relationship with truth and knowledge. To his good fortune, Cornel West had access to professors at Princeton who nurtured a fecund mind in preparation for battle with theoretical forces that diminish Black value, selfhood, worth, and esteem. A method to the xenophobic and white-supremacist madness during the late seventies and early eighties calls West to a vocation of intellectual service. In the introduction to the 1991 publication of *The Ethical Dimensions of Marxist Thought*, West's autobiographical sketch of his undergraduate years at Harvard and the two brief years at Princeton, he narrates academic pursuits as important means to more socially ameliorating ends. Philosophical studies, though at moments rigorously analytical, fed a mind hungry to make a difference. With intentionality, he honed in on historicism and the Hegelian Marxist tradition:

> My eye-opening and horizon-broadening encounter with Richard
> Rorty made me an even stronger Wittgensteinian, although with
> gestures toward Dewey. Rorty's historicist turn was like music to
> my ears. . . . My allegiance to the Hegelian Marxist tradition was
> deepened by Sheldon Wolin—the major influence, along with
> Rorty and C. B. MacPherson—on my thought at the time. It was
> during the two short years at Princeton that I became convinced
> that the values of individuality—the sanctity and dignity of all in-
> dividuals shaped in and by communities—and of democracy—as

> a way of life and mode of being-in-the-world, not just a form of governance—were most precious to me.[15]

Later I discuss individuality and radical democracy as integral remedies to the greed, mendacity, and nihilism of what West often calls, "The American Empire." But in his twenties, he's already strategizing his prophetic plans to improve the well-being of "the least of these." No wonder he comes out of the academic gates swinging at conceptual constructs that continue protracted assaults on Black lives. Given his rigorous training in analytical philosophy, along with the influence of Rorty and others, West capably tackles Cartesian-based philosophy on its own terms. With its emphases on foundational truths and certainty, this Cartesian-based epistemology poses a problem for anyone seeking asylum from perils and prisons of mental incarceration. Like W. E. B. Du Bois a generation before him, Cornel West possesses the tools to creatively engage established discourses on truth by establishing philosophical constructs that serve as catalysts for a more pragmatic epistemology. This epistemology includes radical historicism (to a larger extent) and prophetic pragmatism (to a lesser extent). As theoretical tenets informing a Westian epistemology, radical historicism and prophetic pragmatism conceive truth differently than Cartesian-based epistemology. I now turn to these theoretical tenets, which ultimately will be foundational for an ethic of radical freedom. These tenets include the questioning of four positions: questioning objective truth, foundational knowledge for one's beliefs, the truth outside our minds matches what's inside our minds, and that there is a mind capable of accessing knowledge beyond experiences. Though West tackles each of these questions in the span of his nearly forty years of scholarship, his most acute theorizing takes place during the first decade of his career as a scholar.

Radical Historicism: Truth as Fallible and Revisable

Recall earlier how Michael Eric Dyson laments Cornel West's failure to match the scholarship he produced decades ago, and that my reply to this unfair critique is that West, as itinerate public intellectual, now bears the fruits from theoretical labors. Before diving into these deep theoretical waters, I situate the following discussion with a transcript from a brief exposé Cornel West gives on truth in the documentary film *Examined Life*.

15. West, *Ethical Dimensions*, xx.

> [I think of] truth as a way of life, as opposed to a set of propositions
> that correspond to things in the world. Human beings are unable
> to ever gain any monopoly on Truth (capital "T"), we might have
> access to truth (little "t"), but they are fallible claims about truth
> and they could be wrong, and open to revision and so on. So there
> is a certain kind of mystery that goes hand in hand with truth. This
> is why so many existential thinkers, whether they be religious or
> secular . . . have worked to accent our finitude and our inability to
> fully grasp the ultimate nature of reality and truth about things.
> And therefore you talk about truth being tied to the way to truth,
> because once you give up on the notion of fully grasping the way
> the world is, you're gonna talk about what are the ways I can sus-
> tain my quest for truth. How do you sustain a journey, a path,
> toward truth? The way to truth? The truth talk goes hand in hand
> with talk about the way to truth.[16]

This cautionary acceptance, West states above, recognizes that we truth-seekers are fallible creatures, unqualified to access absolute truth. What-ever truths we know are small "t" truth claims. What kind of truth does truth with a small "t" consist of? The answer is, any truth claims that are historically and contextually situated. Only historical and mathematical facts are candidates for Truth, capital "T." Hence, West accounts for what he calls "truth," small "t." The question then is which truth claims we accept and which ones we reject. In the quotation above, the earlier West speaks through the later West, voicing that human fallibility precludes the pos-sibility of Truth, capital "T."

Here our postmodern prophet leaves room for questioning notions presumed to be true. And for the losers of the game of truth, West provides a means to combat mechanisms of oppression precipitated by this game. As a postmodern prophet with post-analytic sensibilities, West provides a practical yet pragmatic conception of truth, while polemically poking at the correspondence theory of truth (which I discuss later). Truth is not a set of propositions that correspond to things in the world, announces West. And though perhaps many watching or listening to this dialogue ap-preciate the implicit humility, anyone casually familiar with West's radical historicism and progressive/prophetic pragmatism will catch the phrases "fallible claims about truth" and "open to revision." These catchphrases sum up the detailed and rigorous philosophical work West wrote on truth four decades ago. Like his hero Socrates who seeks to improve the souls of fellow

16. Taylor, *Examined Life*.

citizens, West, our postmodern circuit rider, provides practical instruction from theoretical insights he wrote decades ago. His lectures at sold-out auditoriums, churches, colleges, and universities improve the collective consciousness of the nation. In the interview from *Examined Life* (from the quotation above), West gives a practical lesson on truth. This lesson is essentially a practical remix of his more philosophic treatment of truth in *The Ethical Dimensions of Marxist Thought*. This brief lesson on truth is not mere philosophical grandstanding; rather, like Socrates before him, West provides a pedagogical pathway for citizens to be and do better. West cautions against attempts at monopolizing truth given that times, culture, and contexts change, thereby reminding us that truth undergoes revisions. This is why West contests presumptions of objective and absolute truth by offering historicism as an alternative to foundationalism.

The radical historicism West puts forth in *The Ethical Dimension of Marxist Thought* requires dismantling foundationalism by demonstrating that foundationalism is a philosophic position that ignores particular modes of existence. Being philosophic means that this version of knowledge and truth seeks to prove the status, objectivity, and validity of moral principles. Rather than seeking for certitude as Cartesians do, the radical historicist understands that knowledge and truth are fallible. According to the religious epistemologist, Nicholas Wolterstorff, the goal of foundationalism is "to form a body of theories from which all prejudice, bias, and unjustified conjecture have been eliminated."[17] Wolterstorff argues that foundationalists attempt to accomplish this by establishing firm foundations of certitude and "build the house of theory on it by methods of whose reliability we are equally certain."[18] Positions like this one posed by Wolterstorff are disadvantageous to those for whom these foundations disfavor. And for Cornel West, the problem is that these foundations are presumed necessarily true without historical and cultural factors.

The first chapter of *The Ethical Dimensions of Marxist Thought* discusses positions of truth that are at polar opposites. These positions are hard objectivism and strong relativism. Hard objectivism asserts that not only does such a thing as objective and absolute truth exist, but that also, we can assess this truth. Absolute or objective truth stands the test of time and changes in cultural values, scientific discoveries, and historical revisions have little bearing on this truth. In his own words and with erudition

17. Wolterstorff, *Reason*, 28.
18. Wolterstorff, *Reason*, 28.

indicative of his Princeton pedigree, West says of absolute truth: "claims it is possible to generate and justify rationally necessary or universally obligatory moral standards against which to judge rival ethical judgments (or beliefs)."[19] This quotation, though convoluted and complicated, if taken seriously, unveils costly moral ramifications, which is to say that any rational appeal to absolute truth will cancel out competing moral claims. Take the earlier example about the moral claim that the rational design for marriage is between a man and a woman. If we believe this is an absolute moral truth, then that's the end of the conversation. But if we examine this position from the perspective of radical historicism, such a claim must be evaluated contextually. When evaluated contextually, West contends that a presumed moral truth about the "design for marriage" has its challenges in these postmodern moments.

West laments positions held by Marx's disciples, Engels, Kautsky, and Lukács, who made the unfortunate move away from the radical historicism of their teacher. West then shows he intends to reconstruct the arguments of Marx's disciples who deviated from the radical historicism of their teacher. As noted earlier, *The Ethical Dimensions of Marxist Thought* is West's doctoral dissertation entitled, "Ethics, Historicism and The Marxist Tradition." In the abstract to the dissertation, West states the following:

> I then critically reconstruct the arguments of three major Marxist thinkers—Engels, Kautsky, and Lukács—who, in their own ways, subscribe to the traditional vision of philosophy. I argue that all three adopt moderate historicism in ethics owing to this subscription, and specifically because of their own particular foundationalist conceptions of epistemology and science. I claim that Engels' teleological quest resembles a Piercian move to preserve the notion of moral objectivity by holding that it amounts roughly to what moral agents will converge to or agree upon in the long run. I claim that Kautsky's naturalistic quest is similar, though less sophisticated, to a Deweyan move that tries to translate norms-talk into needs-talk (or, more specifically instincts-talk) in order to avoid moral relativism. Lastly, I claim that Lukács' ontological quest is a sophisticated Hegelian move to overcome traditional, especially modern positivist foundationalism in epistemology and science only to arrive at a new form of foundationalism—in

19. West, *Ethical Dimensions*, 4.

> science and ethics—in ontological garb. I try to show that these
> three quests for moral objectivity fail.[20]

This quotation is quite telling, because it shows that Marx's disciples made attempts to distance themselves from notions of objective truth and moral absolutes, yet ultimately, found themselves back on the foundationalist road. Opting to travel this road meant a detour from the social philosophy and ethical dimensions of Marxist thought.

The social philosophy of Marx gave considerate credence to how context and historical circumstances contribute to notions of right and wrong. The ethical dimension of Marxist thought eschewed some overarching law or rule when engaging in moral deliberation, ultimately denying the foundationalist's contention of rational necessity of philosophic grounds. In other words, Marx denies foundationalism because it assumes that our moral beliefs come from a foundation accessible to any rational person. Radical historicism says no to moral positions that embrace absolute and objective truth presumed universally rational. To the contrary, radical historicism champions a weak relativist notion of contingent, revisable, and tentative truth claims. West sums up his position regarding radical historicism in a quite consequential quotation:

> The radical historicist discards the pejorative self-description "relativist" and rejects the objectivist lens. The radical historicist does not see attainable or unattainable timeless criteria, necessary grounds, or universal foundations which cut through the flux of history, but rather different dynamic human agreements and disagreements and changing community-specific criteria constituting continuous and discontinuous traditions which are linked in highly complex ways to multiple human needs, interests, biases, aims, goals, and objectives. If there is to be an appropriate response to hard objectivism . . . the radical historicist approach would not be to reject its philosophic status, as does moral relativism, but rather to attempt to understand its historic emergence and its social function and cultural role during its dominance, and to describe and explain its decline.[21]

One of the most consequential books and perhaps his most intensely philosophical is *The American Evasion of Philosophy: A Genealogy of Pragmatism*, a book where West continues the conversation he began in his

20. West, "Ethics, Historicism," ii–iii.
21. West, *Ethical Dimensions*, 12–13.

doctoral dissertation. Still in his twenties and in close historical proximity to his graduate work at Princeton, West continues his critique of Cartesian-based notions of objective truth and indubitable foundations of knowledge. In *The American Evasion of Philosophy*, West furthers this critique, following the lead of Rorty, and others, by deconstructing discourses of "the correspondence theory of truth," "the myth of the given," and "representationalism." The book's title, *The American Evasion of Philosophy* leaves little room for suspicion regarding the polemical posture West assumes. Yet before diving more deeply into the contours of this critique, some attention to how the title accentuates the method West uses.

As the words of the title suggest, this book intends to evade philosophy, which on the surface seems straightforward, but with a pensive pause, one notices an ambiguity. "The American Evasion of" leaves one to wonder which philosophy he intends to evade and how and what does West use to execute this evasion? Does the book evade American philosophy, or does the book show how an America discourse evades philosophy? As convoluted as these questions seem, knowing the object and subject of evasion unveils the direction of this evasion. Is American philosophy evading or is American philosophy the object of evading? My answer to both ambiguous questions, then, is unambiguously yes. Yes, this book uses (progressive) *American* pragmatism to evade *Anglo-American* (analytic) philosophy. The subtitle, though signaling the theoretical work ahead, is also the inaugural publication from and consecration of a postmodern prophet. The words "Genealogy" and "Pragmatism" in this subtitle bespeak the bequeathing of Nietzsche's prefiguration of postmodernity and Rorty's resuscitation of the American pragmatist tradition. Friedrich Nietzsche's *The Genealogy of Morals* pursues an alternative historical assessment of morality by exposing the Judeo-Christian pseudo dichotomy of the notions of good and evil. And Richard Rorty refreshes one American (pragmatism) philosophical tradition against the stale and static notions of truth espoused by another American (analytical) philosophical tradition.

Therefore, in good postmodern fashion, West genealogically reconstructs progressive pragmatism in order to confront social evils and existential threats that preclude well-being.

This genealogy brings into its canon thinkers excluded from American pragmatism proper. Some of these thinkers include Reinhold Niebuhr and W. E. B. Du Bois. Also, by doing a "genealogy of pragmatism," West does three important things. First, he provides a political interpretation of American pragmatism. Second, he provides a social history of ideas, whereby he examines the social, cultural, and intellectual influences of certain philosophers. And third, West employs Emersonian tropes as foundational tools of reconstructing American pragmatism. It is this last reason that has concomitant concerns with West's epistemology. He weaponizes thought to combat the crippling effect Cartesian-based epistemology posed to ordinary people who are the historical losers in the game of truth. For West, Emerson sidesteps Cartesian-style philosophy by placing emphasis on power, provocation, and personality. I discuss these tropes more in reference to West's prophetic outlook of reality, but for now they establish the fact that one's position regarding truth and the acquisition of knowledge comes out of cultural, social, political, and existential realities. West admits that Emerson is not a philosopher per se; yet he contends that Emerson prefigures pragmatism by using rhetorical strategies to explain America to herself. In an important quotation West says that

> he is a cultural critic who devised and deployed a vast array of rhetorical strategies in order to exert intellectual and moral leadership over a significant segment of the educated classes of his day. The rhetorical strategies, principally aimed at explaining America to itself, weave novel notions of power, provocation, and personality into a potent and emerging American ideology of voluntaristic invulnerability and utopian possibility.[22]

Three tropes Emerson employs are power, provocation, and personality. By weaving power, provocation, and personality into prophetic pragmatism, West situates philosophical discourse in general and epistemology in particular to the existential realities of the most vulnerable in society. Vulnerable citizens have the power to determine whether a particular conception of truth takes their experience into consideration; they may also provoke pervasive notions of truth that preclude flourishing; and with personality they have the wherewithal to determine which notions insult racial identity.

The result of this genealogical reconstruction of progressive pragmatism is prophetic pragmatism. Though a theory West conceptualized over thirty years ago is as alive and as relevant as Plato's theory of the forms, Immanuel Kant's categorical imperatives, and James Cone's Black liberation theology. Prophetic pragmatism takes progressive pragmatism to another level of relevance, while, in concert with lessons of his mentors and teachers, continuing to accent themes of the pragmatist tradition. In his critical

---

22. West, *American Evasion of Philosophy*, 10.

evaluation of prophetic pragmatism, Clevis Headley lays out the themes of pragmatism, showing affinities with West's prophetic version:

> Despite its contest-ability, we can isolate core themes of pragmatism. First, prophetic pragmatists reject the idea that philosophy needs secure, fixed foundations that can be known with absolute certainty. This view presents pragmatism's commitment to anti-foundationalism, although not all foundationalists are pragmatists. Indeed, pragmatists generally do not believe that any form of inquiry rests upon sure, secured, and *a priori* foundations. In conjunction with antifoundationalism, pragmatism also advocates a contextual conception of reality and values. Second, pragmatism embraces fallibilism. Believing that all inquiry is fallible, pragmatists tend to adopt a certain epistemological liberalism, which acknowledges that each knowledge claim is subject to revision or, rather, is not immune to criticism.[23]

Among the many points made by Headley, implicitly important here is consistency in conversation that espouses a truth that is infallible, subject to revision, and that potentially changes depending on historical and contextual conditions. But as with any body of work or accumulation of influences, West's prophetic pragmatism has antecedent influences ever keeping us mindful that he is a post-analytic philosopher turned postmodern prophet. We work backwards and access the post-analytic resources of Cornel West's epistemological arsenal. These resources remain indelible and integral in most if not all of any philosophical work West produced. Which means we are back to Rorty but for different reasons we explored earlier with radical historicism. Along with Rorty we have two more post-analytic philosophers, W. V. O. Quine and Wilfrid Sellars. These philosophers occasion what West calls in *The American Evasion of Philosophy* the resurgence of progressive pragmatism, which West admits, clears philosophical space for remaining tenets of West's epistemology: anti-realism/anti-representationalism, and "Demythologizing the Myth of the Given." We go back to Rorty.

23. Headley, "Cornel West on Prophesy," 61–62.

West's Epistemology: Anti-Realism/Anti-Representationalism, and "Demythologizing the Myth of the Given"

One of Rorty's criticisms is that moral reasoning came from the conviction that reality consisted of "the given" and "objective truth." He relies on Sellars and Quine. He uses Sellars' critique of "the given"[24] and Quine's attack on traditional empiricism,"[25] resulting in Rorty's version of anti-representationalism.[26] In the preface to *Philosophy and the Mirror of Nature*, Rorty reveals his dependence on and appreciation for the works of Sellars and Quine:

> Sellars's attack on the Myth of the Given seemed to me to render doubtful the assumptions behind most of modern philosophy. Still later, I began to take Quine's skeptical approach to the language-fact distinction seriously, and to try to combine Quine's point of view with Sellars's. Since then, I have been trying to isolate more of the assumptions behind the problematic of modern philosophy, in the hope of generalizing and extending Sellars's and Quine's criticisms of traditional empiricism. Getting back to these assumptions, and making clear that they are optional, I believe, would be "therapeutic" in the way in which Carnap's original dissolution of standard textbook problems was "therapeutic." This book is the result of that attempt.[27]

It is arguably the case that many analytic philosophers embrace a realist view of reality. This realist view embraces acute positivism because, like positivism, realism (realism as it pertains to truth and true statements) claims that linguistic items verify objective reality.[28] This is to say that realists contend that the only reliable language is language that is empirically verifiable, and that true statements stand in representational relation to mind-independent reality. The position held by some realists is that only statements of physics can respond to "facts of the matter."[29] Rorty's anti-realism discounts this position and argues instead that reality is more involved

---

24. See Sellars, "Empiricism."

25. See Quine, *From a Logical Point of View*.

26. See Rorty, *Philosophy and the Mirror of Nature*.

27. Rorty, *Philosophy and the Mirror of Nature*, xiv.

28. See Rorty's discussion of realism in *Objectivity, Relativism, and Truth*, 2.

29. Rorty, *Philosophy and the Mirror of Nature*, 2.

and complicated. He contends that thoughts about the world are detached from neither our context nor our bodies:

> The anti-representationalist is quite willing to grant that our language, like our bodies, has been shaped by the environment we live in. Indeed, he or she insists on this point—the point that our minds or our language could not (as the representationalist skeptic fears) be "out of touch with the reality" any more than our bodies could. What he or she denies is that it is explanatorily useful to pick and choose among the contents of our minds or our language and say that this or that item "corresponds to" or "represents" the environment in a way that some other item does not.[30]

Rorty's anti-representationalism took the philosophical world by storm and served as the impetus for pragmatism's resurgence. The publication of *Philosophy and the Mirror of Nature* dealt a serious blow to mainstream analytic philosophy. By pointing out the weaknesses of representationalism (or realism as it is later called), Rorty made a good case for the resurgence of American pragmatism, with its emphasis on experimentation, fallibilism, and social practices. American pragmatism places emphasis on experimentation, instrumentalism, and politics, and it proves to be a tool of liberation and amelioration from human malignancies. Cornel West highlights pragmatism's ameliorative impulse when he compares it to Anglo-American (i.e., analytic) philosophy:

> It is no accident that American pragmatism once again rises to the surface of North Atlantic intellectual life at the present moment. For its major themes of evading epistemology-centered philosophy, accenting human powers, and transforming antiquated modes of social hierarchies in light of religious and/or ethical ideals make it relevant and attractive. The distinctive appeal of American pragmatism in our postmodern moment is its unashamedly moral emphasis and its unequivocally ameliorative impulse. In this world-weary period of pervasive cynicisms, nihilisms, terrorisms, and possible extermination, there is a longing for norms and values that can make a difference, a yearning for principled resistance and struggle that can change our desperate plight.[31]

Rorty's pragmatism no doubt energizes West's avid antagonism of rational foundations for objective truth, but philosophers W. V. O . Quine,

---

30. Rorty, *Philosophy and the Mirror of Nature*, 5.
31. West, *American Evasion of Philosophy*, 4.

Nelson Goodman, and Wilfrid Sellars provide some input as well. West gives these philosophers credit for their critical contributions to evading Cartesian-style epistemology in *The American Evasion of Philosophy*, but he also gives attention to these philosophers and their critical assessments in other earlier essays. Two are worthy of elucidation. They are "Nietzsche's Prefiguration of Postmodern Philosophy" and the other is an essay titled, "A Philosophical View of Easter."

"Nietzsche's Prefiguration of Postmodern Philosophy" examines the philosophies of W. V. O. Quine, Nelson Goodman, Wilfrid Sellars, and Richard Rorty. All four philosophers are important for occasioning the move against the Cartesian-based philosophy that was pervasive during the early and middle periods of the twentieth century. Not surprisingly, the three philosophical moves West portrays are:

> the move toward antirealism or conventionalism in ontology; the move toward the demythologization of the myth of the given or anti-foundationalism in epistemology; and the move toward the detranscendentalization of the subject or the dismissal of the mind as a sphere of inquiry.[32]

Regarding realism, West offers a two-pronged definition. The first prong links realism to the correspondence theory, where there is a distinction made between "ideas and objects, words and things, sentences and states of affair, or theories and the world."[33] The second prong "proposes something other than human social practice to serve as the final court of appeal determining what is and what we ought to believe."[34] Two of the most noted proponents of pervasive modes of analytic style epistemology are Rudolf Carnap and A. J. Ayer. Carnap in his *Logical Construction of the World* argues that one acquires knowledge by reducing statements about the world to immediate experience (phenomenalism).[35] A. J. Ayer published his *Language, Truth, and Logic* (1936) in which he argues that the only meaningful statements are those that are empirically verifiable.[36]

West points out that Goodman and Quine brilliantly deconstruct and dismantle positions espoused by Carnap and Ayer. Goodman problematizes Carnap's phenomenalism by highlighting the difficulty of reducing

32. West, *Cornel West Reader*, 414.

33. West, *Cornel West Reader*, 190.

34. West, *Cornel West Reader*, 190.

35. West, *Cornel West Reader*, 190.

36. West, *Cornel West Reader*, 190.

reality to mere observation and empirical experience. In other words, truth and knowledge, for Goodman, is not a matter of what we can prove empirically. Rather, truth and knowledge are a matter of what fits one's reality. Or as West puts it, "Truth of a hypothesis after all is a matter of fit—fit with a body of theory, and fit of hypothesis and theory to the data at hand and the fact to be encountered."[37] Quine disagrees with Ayer's notion of empirical verification by arguing that it is difficult to reduce statements of the world to empirical proof. Quine essentially argues that statements about the world are not done empirically but are done by examining competing theories of the world. And "competing theories (versions or descriptions) of the world, not isolated statements," vary regarding the truth-value of statements that make up these theories of the world.[38] West lets Quine speak for himself in this regard:

> If this view is right, it is misleading to speak of the empirical content of an individual statement—especially if it is a statement at all remote from the experiential periphery of the field. Furthermore it becomes folly to seek a boundary between synthetic statements, which hold contingently on experience, and analytic statements, which hold come what may. Any statement can be held true come what may, if we make drastic enough adjustments elsewhere in the system. Even a statement very close to the periphery can be held true in the face of recalcitrant experience by pleading hallucination or by amending certain statements of the kind called logical laws. Conversely, by the same token, no statement is immune to revision.[39]

The background behind this quotation is Quine's critique of the Kantian position that all analytic judgments are known *a priori*, whereas synthetic judgments require empirical verification. Quine's breakthrough proves that there is really no difference between analytic and synthetic judgments and that both judgments come from experience. Of course, Quine's critique carries over to Ayer as well. Attempting to carry on the Kantian argument, Quine notes that Ayer's verification theory of truth poses the same problem as Kant's analytic/synthetic distinction, namely that our experiences of the world inform our theories of the world. West suggests

---

37. West, *Cornel West Reader*, 192. Further discussions of Goodman's work are found in the following: Goodman, *Ways of Worldmaking*.

38. West, *Cornel West Reader*, 192.

39. Quine, *Word and Object*, 43.

that Rorty too chimes in on this critique against Ayer and the verification theory of truth. According to West, Rorty concludes

> that the theory-laden character of observations relativizes talk about the world such that appeals to "the world" as a final court of appeal to determine what is true or what we should believe is viciously circular. We cannot isolate "the world" from theories of the world, then compare these theories of the world with a theory-free world.[40]

The epistemological bottom line for Quine, Goodman, Rorty, and West is that notions of truth come out of the different ways people may see and experience the world. And given that perspectives differ, truth claims are relative at worst and contextual at best.

The second point of departure that these postmodern philosophers take is a move away from foundationalism, which is the conviction that there are basic beliefs undergirding the rational process. The official argument against foundationalism is what West presents as "Demythologizing the Myth of the Given." The following is how West describes this myth:

> The Myth of the Given roughly holds that there is a given element—a self-justifying, intrinsically credible, theory-neutral, non-inferential element—in experience that provides the foundations for other knowledge claims and serves as the final terminating points for chains of epistemic justification.[41]

Postmodern philosophers who explicitly demythologize this are Rorty and Wilfrid Sellars. It is Sellars' psychological nominalism that intends to deconstruct this myth. This deconstruction suggests that proponents of the "Myth of the Given" confuse the difference between "how one acquires knowledge" and "how one goes about justifying the knowledge one acquires."[42] For Sellars, this confusion dissolves once one realizes that knowledge actually "begins with the ability to justify."[43] Sellars also contends that there is no such thing as prelinguistic awareness. "That all awareness—of abstract and particular entities—is a linguistic affair."[44]

40. West, *Cornel West Reader*, 193.

41. West, *Cornel West Reader*, 198.

42. West, *Cornel West Reader*, 200.

43. West, *Cornel West Reader*, 200.

44. West, *Cornel West Reader*, 200.

Rorty builds on Sellars' psychological nominalism with epistemological behaviorism. This epistemological behaviorism contends that the acquisition of knowledge is a result of intersubjective and social interaction. Both Rorty and Sellars note that the quest of epistemic certainty is a fruitless endeavor and that any presumption of a "given" in the rational process is a misunderstanding made by modern philosophy.[45]

The third and final notion is the decentralizing of the subject and is, as West suggests, a natural consequence of anti-realism and anti-foundationalism.[46] With this notion, postmodern philosophers grapple with the inherited Cartesian notion of the "ghost in machines," which proposes an isolated disembodied "ego." This ego (or more appropriately, cogito) is a self-contained sphere of inquiry, which does not rely on context, social realities, and local communities for cognitive input.

The philosophers who offer a detranscendentalization of the subject are Quine and Rorty. Quine essentially argues that mental states are formed under specific circumstances. Underlying this viewpoint, West believes, is Quine's conviction that "there simply are no mental states, but rather neural events."[47] Rorty builds on Quine's version of this detranscendentalization by completely eliminating the notion of a mind/body dualism. As noted earlier, Rorty believes that the mind and the body depend on each other for the acquisition of knowledge. That is, there is no such thing as a mind-independent reality. And moreover, the mind and body depend on social and cultural practices to help construct consciousness.[48]

Although West attempts to make a case for these three philosophical movements, he also argues that Nietzsche precedes Quine, Rorty, Goodman, and Sellars by problematizing the epistemological presumptions of both objective truth and indubitable ahistorical acontextual knowledge. However, West suggests that Nietzsche's point of departure is that mere critique of objective truth and the Cartesian project results in nihilism if there is no alternative conceptual replacement. Near the end of the essay West makes the following observation:

> For Nietzsche, this nihilism results from certain ideals of modern Europe, especially those ideals that presuppose belief in the categories of "aim," "unity," and "truth." Nihilism is a natural

45. West, *Cornel West Reader*, 200.
46. West, *Cornel West Reader*, 205.
47. West, *Cornel West Reader*, 206.
48. West, *Cornel West Reader*, 206.

consequence of a culture (or civilization) ruled and regulated by categories that mask manipulation, mastery, and domination of peoples and nature.[49]

Ultimately, West hopes that the deconstruction offered by these postmodern philosophers would have a replacement or at least have a constructive counter-movement. And although West also embraces anti-realism, anti-foundationalism, and decentralization of the subject, he sees room for a more robust and relevant epistemology.

West continues the epistemological conversation in the brilliant and creative essay, "A Philosophical View of Easter," and in *The Ethical Dimensions of Marxist Thought*, and his *The American Evasion of Philosophy*. These writings grapple with the problems of objective truth and the grounding of philosophic knowledge, ultimately resulting in a theory of radical historicism and prophetic pragmatism.

In "A Philosophical View of Easter" West explores aspects of the resurrection with regard to its truth-value, epistemic status, and significance.[50] This essay is not an apologetic approach to understanding the resurrection, thereby attempting to show that resurrection claims are true. Neither is it a religious manifesto attempting to adjudicate witnesses who affirmed the resurrection as a historical reality. Rather, it is a creative approach to epistemologically engage resurrection claims. Specifically West raises the following epistemological questions: "What does it mean to say that the resurrection is true?" "How do we know that it is true?" and "What significance does the resurrection's truth claim have for Christians?"[51]

To answer these questions, West locates the discourse in the context of our claims about the self, world, and God. For West, these claims come from theories that promote various conceptions of the self, world, and God, and these theories vary depending on the metaphysical, existential, and epistemological posture of the theorist. What this means for West is that truth-value for a proposition in question is examined in light of a particular discursive field. Hence, a claim that a particular proposition is true must take into consideration how people think and believe in a local context.

Regarding the resurrection, West thinks that it is helpful to start with the belief system of those claiming the resurrection to be true, especially those disciples who are responsible for its proliferation. West wants to

49. West, *Cornel West Reader*, 208.

50. West, "Philosophical View of Easter," 415–20.

51. West, "Philosophical View of Easter," 415.

know, "What are the conditions of their belief?" "What consensus about the resurrection claims does the community have?" In answering these questions, West thinks that philosophers must analyze truth-value of statements through certain theories about the world, self, and God. One theory is the correspondence theory of truth. In his essay on Easter, West calls the correspondence theory of truth a commonsensical view that argues a "claim is true or false if it can be correlated with a particular set of experiences or observations such that all and only members of that set are evidence for or against the claim."[52]

For West, the correspondence theory of truth problematizes any particular claim because that claim is based on a presumption of objective reality, namely, that reality to which it corresponds. West sees two problems regarding this position as it pertains to the resurrection claim. First, the resurrection claim relies on the testimony of disciples who have something to gain by making the claim. And, although West sees no problem with the subjectivity of the claim, he mostly questions presumptions of objectivity based on the claim. In other words, if the disciples thought that the notion of the resurrection corresponds to actual fact, namely that Jesus rose from the dead, then that correspondence makes the resurrection an objective fact. Hence the truth of the resurrection as conceived by the disciples is universal, meaning that every person, regardless of context, must accept the resurrection as true. West sees the correspondence theory of truth to be problematic simply because truth claims are essentially based on experience and not on an objective phenomenon.

The second problem West sees with the claim is its reliance on what is known in contemporary epistemology as the "dogma of sentential reductionism." This dogma contends "sentences have their evidence for or against their truth or falsity isolated from and independent of other sentences."[53] In his polemic against this dogma, West relies on Kuhn and Quine. West shows how these philosophers argue that

> the truth-value of our claims about the self, world and God are determined by marshaling evidence for or against the descriptions, versions or theories of which these claims are a part. This insight leads us to "examine the truth-value of particular versions

---

52. West, "Philosophical View of Easter," 415.
53. West, "Philosophical View of Easter," 416.

> or theories of the self, world, and God, not isolated claims or sentences within these particular descriptions, versions or theories.[54]

West contends that when applied to scientific statements, this dogma reduces statements to equivalent ones consisting solely of observation terms. For West, this approach falls short because the most important sentences within scientific discourse contain terms that cannot be observed (e.g., dispositional terms, metrical terms, and theoretical terms).[55] Another problem West sees with this dogma is that it presumes that these sentences and terms are analyzed in isolation. That is to say, that all descriptions or theories, whether religious or scientific, are understood and analyzed within a context that determines its truth-value. Therefore, the truth-value of the resurrection claims is contingent on the truth-value of particular Christian descriptions or theories of the self, world, and God. And what religious and scientific knowledge have in common is that "both consist of social practices and human activities with different aims to achieve and different problems to address."[56] Truth-values within both religious and scientific discourses have no ultimate court of appeal but are determined by descriptions and theories of the self, world, and God, and these theories and descriptions are penultimate courts of appeal.

For West, there is a convergence between his philosophical leanings and his Christian (Kierkegaardian) sensibilities and that is the profound awareness of our human fallenness and frailty. With this convergence in mind West makes the following confession:

> By accepting a particular (i.e., Kierkegaardian) Christian description and therefore, accenting our fallenness, I am led to adopt a radical historicist view that renders all "truth-talk" a contextual affair, always related to human aims and human problems, human groups and human communities.[57]

This position regarding truth-value, as it pertains to theories of self, world, and God, is the impetus for West's radical historicism. West contends that theories are important because they provide descriptions of how we see and understand the world.

54. West, "Philosophical View of Easter," 416.
55. West, "Philosophical View of Easter," 416.
56. West, "Philosophical View of Easter," 418.
57. West, "Philosophical View of Easter," 418.

Although West makes a brilliant argument, he does walk a kind of conceptual tightrope. On the one hand, he understands truth talk as contextual, yet he wants to deny outright that he is a (strong) relativist. Rosemary Cowan suggests that West backs himself into a corner by eschewing notions of objective truth while at the same time claiming to be a Christian. This position is problematic in that Christian belief systems are grounded in some presumptions of objective truth, and for West to embrace Christianity, he seemingly subscribes to some notions of objective truth. In "A Philosophical View of Easter," radical historicism is West's way to mitigate the ambiguity of conflicting truth claims. Unlike hard objectivism, radical historicism makes no claims of objective truth. And unlike strong relativism, radical historicism fails to embrace an "anything goes" ethic. In *The Ethical Dimensions of Marxist Thought*, West questions ethical positions that presume "ready made" or "objective" foundations from which moral reasoning takes place. He proposes "the radical historicism approach to ethical claims that the search for philosophic criteria, grounds, or foundations is doomed."[58] West further argues that the radical historicist "calls into question the very possibility of an ethics (Kantian ethics, for example) that claims to rest upon philosophic notions of rational necessity and/or universal obligation."[59]

Speaking Truth to Power and Truth without Power

Anyone familiar with Cornel West recalls his prophetic mantra is "to let truth speak," and this speaking gives voice to the most vulnerable to address and hold accountable forces of power; yet paradoxically, power here references a means to speak truth without really addressing the Truth, capital "T," that those who have power possess. Over and over, venue after venue, audience after audience, the postmodern prophet admonishes no one possesses a monopoly on Truth. To be sure, no one can boast of a special endowment of truth claims and thanks to West, radical historicism, and prophetic pragmatism, we understand the fallibility of truth and know that it always requires revision. Left out of this calculus is the subconscious acceptance or perhaps even the conscious acquiescence of pervasive notions of Truth, capital "T." Cornel West provides practical assurance of our God-given right to speak truth to power and by extension, exercise our

58. West, *Ethical Dimensions*, 1.
59. West, *Ethical Dimensions*, 1.

democratic privilege to confront power. Unfortunately, this nascent naïveté underestimates the Truth power (forces) possesses.

Given the symbiotic relationship between practice and theory, West's recent attention to truth-telling animates the philosophical renditions of radical historicism and pragmatic truth West espoused in his earlier philosophical texts. To this extent, the practical prophetic West who sermonizes on truth exposes limitations on the theoretic construct of radical historicism. Limitations of practical truth go back to the very language of theoretic truth. In his essay "'Radical Historicism,' Anti-philosophy, and Marxism," John Pittman argues that the adjective "radical" modifying "historicism," overstates Marx's notion of historicism. Yes, Karl Marx embraced historicism, Pittman agrees, but the adjective "radical" lacks historical precedence (no pun intended). In other words, Cornel West imposes "radical" on Marx. Pittman suggests that one "will not find these terms and conceptions in Marx, or in the other Young Hegelians, or in Hegel."[60] Indeed, even if Marx never depicts his version of historicism as radical, what's clear is that West believes in a historicism with radical expressions. To be radical, then, means advocating for a version of truth that considers one's background, consensus among members of a particular community, and understanding that versions and notions of truth have historical importance and relevance. But the question is, does any of this make it radical? I suggest that it makes historicism potentially radical in thought though not necessarily radical in practice.

Being potentially radical implies limitations, which reflects less on Pittman's observations and more on an absentee asset, and that is *power*. Both West's radical historicism and pragmatic conception of truth pose a paradoxical problem; namely, courageous consciousness that speaks "truth to power," misses, at least comprehensively, power's relation to truth. Yes, prophetic and pragmatic truth-telling requires courage, no doubt subjecting one to physical, professional, and personal harm. And say what you want about West's current scholarship, you will have to agree that this postmodern and post-analytic philosopher never ceases to occupy his prophetic post and watch. Just listen or watch any speech, lecture, symposium, you name it, Cornel West consistently combines a calculus of theory and praxis, thereby infusing empathy for the "least of these." Yet, his brand of truth, small "t," is more about character than content. Speaking truth, small "t," inspires allies and perhaps frustrates foes; however, Truth, capital "T,"

60. Pittman, "'Radical Historicism,'" 226.

remains an existential weapon of mass destruction. Oppression's long and enduring narrative depends on the consent of its victims who champion harmful notions of truth they conceive as absolute. And even those who know better may choose silence for fear of professional paralysis and a crippling of career progression. The latter resembles Foucault's notion of "docile bodies," where he shows, in his genealogical book *Discipline and Punish*, the emasculating control *power* has on the proliferation of pervasive Truth. Theoretical formulations like radical historicism and pragmatic conceptions of truth alert us "truth" changes over time (historical) and across cultures (contextual), but to say very little about power leaves these constructs wanting. My purpose is to build on the theoretical formulations West established early in his career, which, for constructing a postmodern ethic of radical freedom, requires reconstructing radical historicism and prophetic pragmatic truth. Below discusses the limitation of these theoretical constructs in more detail.

The task for radical historicism is theoretic because it takes into consideration the general consensus about God, self, and the world. Radical historicism espouses a notion of truth that is fluid and always subject to change. When the task of ethics is theoretic, its role is to:

> discover ways in which to develop a larger consensus and community, such as through example and exposure, through pressure and persuasion, without the idea of a last philosophic court of appeal in the background. If one disagrees with a particular consensus or community, the task is not to seek philosophic foundations for one's view, but rather to put forward a realizable alternative, a new possibility for consensus and community, and then to make it attractive to others.[61]

The theoretic task of ethics is to consider judgments people make about the world, self, and God and how these judgments inform notions of truth. Regarding discourse on truth, what is of crucial importance is the location of truth and not some Archimedean point. As West notes in his essay on the resurrection, truth is a contextual affair and derives out of that the beliefs a particular community has about the world, self, and God. The radical historicist argues that truth is a consequence of the contingent community and community-specific agreements relative to particular norms, goals, and objectives of the community in question.

---

61. West, *Ethical Dimensions*, 1.

Part I: Practical Conditions for the Possibility of a Postmodern Ethic

The Ethical Dimensions of Marxist Thought, as many know by now, is a revision of Cornel West's PhD dissertation, "Ethics, Historicism and the Marxist Tradition," and similar to my personal experiences noted earlier, West also wrestles with contradictions and paradoxes of influential Christian doctrines that promote truth claims that preclude well-being. With these contradictions in mind, West tackles conjectures of truth on two fronts, namely conservative Christian parochialism and myopia, and tenets of Cartesian-based epistemology. *The Ethical Dimensions of Marxist Thought* is an erudite answer to the existential crises perpetrated by contemporary epistemology by imposing truth and belief claims that do more damage than good—if any good at all. And despite occasional thin critiques of the Baptist faith he often lauds, *The Ethical Dimensions of Marxist Thought* implicitly casts a shadow on the paralyzing pronouncements of that faith. Rosemary Cowan highlights West's rejection of epistemological certainty, while also tethering existentially problematic claims championed by conservative Christians. Cowan asserts:

> In being wary of traditional Christian conceptions of Truth, West does not go so far as to reject truth altogether, nor does he lapse into relativism. What he does reject is the epistemological certainty that some Christians ascribe to their interpretation of the Bible, whereby they claim to know the Truth and reject interpretations that differ from theirs as, quite simply, wrong. Here some might detect a paradox, as West himself states unequivocally that the Christian Right are mistaken in their interpretation of the Bible.[62]

Cowan notices the balancing act West performs by valorizing the prophetic Christian virtues while rejecting the objective truth many Christians, especially conservatives, embrace. Arguably, the Shiloh Baptist Church of West's childhood lacks the extreme dogmatism of Avondale Church of Christ. However, both churches appeal to the Bible as the literal word of God and consequently, appeal to a Divine source for ultimate truth, and whether he admits it or not, West embraces a notion of truth that presumes a standard by which to govern behavior. This makes truth objective for a particular cultural or historical context. Because of that I see West's radical historicism, although helpful, by itself too dogmatic for a postmodern ethic of radical freedom. Again, what makes radical historicism radical if it cosigns on some appeal to objectivity? Pittman puts the concern another way

62. Cowan, *Cornel West*, 69.

and suggests that West ends up doing what he is trying to prevent, namely, eschew metanarratives and impose rational necessity on one's beliefs:

> Of course, here we are in danger of redeploying the kind of "metanarrative," replete with its own version of rational necessity that would consign the whole project to the discredited lineage of those bad, grand philosophical systems. Not so "radical" historicism, after all![63]

In public speeches, to include the first one I attended, West lamented the tendency to lump all Black people into one homogeneous blob. Yet, he contends that good theory of truth is one that takes into consideration the values and beliefs espoused by a local community—safeguarding that community from irrelevant truth claims. In "A Philosophical View of Easter," West sets the stage for radical historicism by deconstructing the "correspondence theory of truth," showing that a good theory of truth must take into consideration a community's conception of the self, world, and God. The correspondence theory of truth assigns an objective status to beliefs, contending that there should be a correspondence between beliefs and reality. For West, no such thing is possible, and West suggests that a good theory of truth must consider the conditions, context, and consensus of a local community's beliefs. Truth claims regarding the resurrection is a good case in point. Truth claims of the resurrection come out of the conditions, context, and consensus of a particular community; namely, those disciples putting forth resurrection claims. In this case, there is a notion of truth, but this notion does not extend beyond the community of believers who may appreciate these claims and moreover for whom such claims will not do harm to their quality of life. Therefore, while these claims may be truthful to that community, they are not universally applicable to communities everywhere. Recall in *The Ethical Dimensions of Marxist Thought*, where West denies hard objectivism but accepts weak relativism. Hard objectivism that objective reality and moral truths affirm are on par with scientific truths. West denies this position because despite advances in science, truth has cultural and historical value and potentially changes over time. But respectfully, West may want the benefit of having his cake and eating it too. There is consensus from within a context, which may make truth look a bit objective for that context. Yet, he refuses to make the discourse on truth a completely relative affair, conceding that radical historicism is akin to

---

63. Pittman, "'Radical Historicism,'" 230.

what he calls weak relativism. He believes this affinity with weak relativism safeguards his form of ethics from being nihilistic while at the same time denying moral truths commensurate with absolute standards that govern behavior. In other words, West thinks there has to be some notion of truth otherwise we will be left with an "anything goes" ethical agenda. Additionally, he warns against imposing objective standards on everyone. Hence he opts for a safe retreat, namely, weak relativism, which poses a standard but just not one that is universally applicable. And to hold onto "contextual" objective standards of truth, authorizes, to some extent, dogmatism and pietistic posturing.

Take, for example, Cornel West's unambiguous critique of former president Barack Obama, where West not only provides a dogmatic critique of Obama, but does it dogmatically. I get it, and West has company among leftist politicians and intellectuals who see Obama embracing liberal optimistic ideals that improve life for the middle class while the underclass still begs for social and economic crumbs. But it's one thing to disagree with Obama's policies, its another thing to provide a lopsided, scathing critique that may appear pious and self-righteous. I may also add West's disingenuousness. In his 2021 interview with Cornel West, Eduardo Mendieta probes intently into West's disappointment with President Obama, where the former describes Obama as an impediment to democracy. West gives particular attention to Obama's bailout of Wall Street elites, his inattention to the poor, and usage of drones in the Middle East, among other things. To critique Obama is par for the course, but I wonder, why such a harsh and dogmatic critique? Perhaps an answer one may offer in West's defense is that perhaps West is simply doing what prophets do, which is provide polemical and critical commentary on politically harming behavior despite Obama's race. Though paradoxically, it's because of Obama's race that West is unrelenting in his critique. In the same interview, West compares Obama with Martin Luther King, which at best compares a president with a preacher (unfair), or at worst, West holds Obama to a higher standard because he is Black (dogmatic). One of the most interesting things to me is that West publicly chastises the first African American president for what appears to be economic elitism and international insensitivity vis-à-vis drone strikes in the Middle East. Yet he lauds the democratic fervor of Thomas Jefferson and expresses admiration for the philosopher David Hume; both of whom make Barack Obama look like Mother Teresa on her best day. Thomas Jefferson owned slaves, unapologetically stating that Black people are intellectually inferior. David Hume, in similar racist fashion, wrote on more than one occasion asserting Black inferiority, and I am sure endorsed slavery. Yet, the practical rendering of West's radical historicism is to provide a strong objectivist critique of Obama, while providing a weak relativist critique (if that) of outright racist, sexist, and elite white men. My purpose here is not to promote political or racial apologetics, but to show how the danger of making truth contextually and historically objective is just as dangerous as the truth radical historicism interrogates.

Back to the very impetus of my need to promote an ethic of radical freedom, namely, the position of the Avondale Church of Christ, and my friend, who viscerally claimed: "the truth is the truth." Even tenets of contextual and historical truths can be just as oppressive as the truth radical historicism seeks to replace. What West does not take into consideration are the forces of power that are at work within each historical and cultural context. Take, as an example, the forces at work with the advent of Black liberation theology. Although James Cone, Deotis Roberts, and Albert Cleage constructed a version of liberation theology that exposes the power latent within dominant classical theology, it took womanist theology to expose the power latent within Black (that is male Black) theology. The point I make with this brief tangent is that all truth (whether contextual or absolute) is a result of power/knowledge relations.

West's radical historicism is foundational for a postmodern ethic of radical freedom; radical historicism's limited analysis of the powers that influence the emergence of truth. Indeed, radical historicism helps, because it alerts us that truth is hardly objective and absolute, but, ultimately, it is incomplete. Therefore, I begin with this incomplete assessment of truth for a postmodern ethic of radical freedom. I think at this point, Michel Foucault's genealogical method enhances radical historicism. In doing so we see power influences contextual truth (that is, *their* contextual truth), opening up for what I will later call radical epistemology.

Chapter 4

Cornel West and Improvisational Metaphysics

Some may say that it is philosophically problematic and an overstatement to call the metaphysics of Cornel West improvisational. Or that I am taking liberties to even say there is such a thing as a "metaphysics of Cornel West." But this depends on how one defines metaphysics and from what traditions that definition comes. For example, for the analytical tradition, metaphysics emphasizes the ways language and logic describe, depict, and reference things in the world. Then there are the more theological commitments that interpret metaphysics as anything discussing spiritual phenomena. Despite these specific perspectives, a more helpful inquiry to consider the contours of metaphysics more broadly. From there I can offer a conception of what I call, the metaphysics of Cornel West.

Working Definition of Metaphysics?

As I noted above, one's particular philosophical, and I'll add theological, posture determines how one situates a discourse in metaphysics. In ancient Greek philosophy, the word "metaphysics" comprises two words. The first is meta (after) and the second is physics, which quite simply means "after" physics. The preposition "after" implies notions and ideas that are beyond the physical realm or as Aristotle describes as "being qua being."

In other words, metaphysics includes existence and the space in which we exist, whether physically or spiritually. Therefore, broadly speaking, if asked, "What is your metaphysics?" the question is, "What are your positions on God, the self, time, space, infinity, and so on?" In a word, your metaphysics is your view of reality. In an essay, "Relation of Metaphysics and Theology," Paul Tillich discounts metaphysics as a discourse on transcendental ideas or objects existing beyond the physical. In a lengthy but helpful quotation Tillich notes:

> There are two problematic factors, which must be considered in every definition of metaphysics, the first of which was effective for a long time, the other only recently. Metaphysics has suffered under the unjustified connotation that the "meta" in metaphysics points to a realm above the physical realm. This connotation was strongly supported by the Latin word "supranatural," which designated the realm of the divine above nature. Finally the term "experience" in its empiricistic application pushed metaphysics into the role of a "speculation" without an experiential basis. Against these distortions metaphysics should be defined as the analysis of those elements in the encountered reality which belong to its general structure and make experience universally possible. Metaphysics then is the rational inquiry into the structure of being, its polarities and categories as they appear in man's encounter with reality.[1]

Tillich's analysis depicts metaphysics as a rational discourse on the structure of being and humankind's encounter with reality. In working our way to Cornel West and the idea of his improvisational metaphysics, the litmus test is always the ordinary everyday experience of ordinary everyday people. For West, as with Tillich, metaphysical discourse must engage the realities of suffering, oppression, and inferiority. For Tillich it is the job of theology to answer the questions implied in the human condition. West's metaphysics grapples primarily with African American existence in North America to include threats to being, pejorative objectification, and the proclivity to transform what is to what ought to be.

In *Cornel West & Philosophy: The Quest for Social Justice*, Clarence Sholé Johnson, building an argument for Cornel West's metaphysics, notes that historical precedence wrestles with two options. The first option is to value our rational beliefs regardless of our experiences, which philosophers call rationalism. In other words, only what we think about reality matters,

---

1. Tillich, "Relation of Metaphysics and Theology," 57–58.

without the aid of experience. The second is the opposite, which states that only our experiences matter and in fact, how we think about reality comes directly from experiences. Philosophers call this position rationalism. Describing both positions, Johnson states:

> Thus, the issue between the rationalists and the empiricists was about the method by which knowledge of reality could be attained—whether through the employment of reason unaided by experience or through atomistic sensation. According to West, this unresolvable issue that engaged the European philosophers provided, indeed constituted, the point of departure for pragmatism, the only Western philosophy native to America.[2]

It is this notion of "philosophy native to America" that makes all the difference for West. For him, philosophical inquiry, engagement, and discourse must have relevance particularly to the American context. The age-old debate about what we think and our experiences is a useless one without taking into consideration social evils like oppression, marginalization, racism, and sexism. Moreover, metaphysics, if it is to be helpful, must consider these things. In fact, in an essay, "Dispensing with Metaphysics in Religious Thought,"[3] printed in his book *Prophetic Fragments: Illuminations of the Crises in American Religion & Culture*, West laments outdated metaphysics. Any view of reality that ignores realties of everyday life is sound and fury signifying nothing.

A culprit here is an academic theological curriculum expressing lofty notions about God, heaven, and Jesus Christ, yet fails to apply these notions with people's everyday realities and practical concerns. West's brand of metaphysics endorses a more pragmatic approach and in a sense resembles what Victor Anderson calls "a minimalist transcendentalism."[4] Contained within this word is "transcend," which means to be or go beyond. Naturally, the question is "be or go beyond what?" Answering this question gestures the difference between minimalist transcendentalism and maximalist transcendentalism. For Anderson, the latter focuses on the divinity of Jesus, eternal life, the indwelling of the Holy Spirit, and so on. Focusing on these realities has significance, and as a Christian, for West to jettison them altogether makes little sense. However, West critiques academic theology for good reason, namely, its preoccupation with systematic questions

2. Johnson, *Cornel West*, 14.

3. West, *Prophetic Fragments*, 267–70.

4. Anderson, "Is Cornel West," 146–47.

concerning the natures of God and Jesus, the so-called kingdom of God, and attributes of the Holy Spirit. And answers to these questions have little importance, absent assessment and amelioration of the crucibles of suffering, displacement, homelessness, domestic terrorism, and violence, and of course racism, sexism, and homophobia. Anderson suggests that West's minimal transcendence or *metaphysics* "comes very close to reducing transcendence into immanence and Christian faith into radical democracy."[5] Though radical democracy captures Cornel West's vision of reality, it only scratches the surface of the robustness of his multifaceted metaphysics. This is to say that the best way to describe West's version of reality and addressing its endemic concerns is his improvisational metaphysics. To this we now turn.

Improvisational Metaphysics

Cornel West is a jazzman of extraordinary genius who leverages philosophical, practical, and prophetic resources to address existential concerns of vulnerable people. As in the case with jazz, West zigzags from one discipline to another, improvising with playwrights like Anton Chekhov, novelists like Toni Morrison, political theorists like Robert Unger, theological ethicists like Reinhold Niebuhr, and others from a myriad of intellectual traditions. But there is a method to this improvisational madness, and that is the amelioration of existential concerns of ordinary people. His response to the weariness of life is a metaphysical one. That is, improving the conditions of ordinary people motivates and energizes West's writings. And his vision of reality is foundational to improving reality. Like his vision of truth, West's prophetic posture informs and inspires his vision of reality (metaphysics). His entire body of work has nuggets from his metaphysics, but two books, *The American Evasion of Philosophy* and *Prophesy Deliverance*, provide the most pronounced theoretical formulations. Getting to these texts is critical in constructing a postmodern ethic of radical freedom, but as methodology has it, I start with his practical metaphysical lessons and work back to his theoretical insights. That being said, I give attention to improvisational renditions, beginning with West's contemporaneous elucidations and applications of Chekhov, Kierkegaard, and the blues.

5. Anderson, "Is Cornel West," 147.

Chekhov, Kierkegaard, and Blues Sensibility

In a 2017 interview with Eduardo Mendieta, West unapologetically calls himself a blues man of the mind, and it is this sensibility that accommodates transcendence from tragedy to laughter. On the one hand, West embraces frailty as a human being who empathizes with communities that know trauma and tragedy. Living the blues is metaphysical and puts the "real" in the word reality. On the other hand, tragedy is real life, yet one transcends tragedy through hope, making it tragic-comic. And thanks to the existential reflections of Chekhov and Kierkegaard, who embrace tragedy while also realizing that social and existential sickness is not "sickness unto death" as a title of one of Kierkegaard's books suggest. In the interview, West reasons how works by poets and playwrights unlock and open doors we enter to enjoy the transcendence that the tragic-comic precipitates:

> I think that I would like to hold on to the language of not just the tragic, but more and more I talk about the tragicomic. . . . That's why Chekhov, and Beckett and Kafka, have come more to the center of my thinking as opposed to, let's say Sophocles, who's part of a great tradition as it were. . . . But it's been more tragicomic. Evil is integral to both conceptions. But because I want to stress this more concretized, ground leveled conception of agency of response to tragedy, you see, I am a blues man in the life of the mind. And the blues is an autobiographical chronicle of a personal catastrophe expressed lyrically in tragicomic terms.[6]

This blues sensibility looks suffering in the face and sustains character under existential pressures without retreating to despair. In fact, we laugh even in the face of tragedy, thereby loosing suffering of its grip.

In the introduction to *The Cornel West Reader*, West notes that three questions just listed should be asked when giving consideration to his vocation as a scholar and to how he understands individuality and radical democracy. To be human is to live with the inevitable realities of death, despair, and disease. Individuals are, as West notes most profanely, "two-legged-linguistically-conscious-creatures-born-between-urine-and-faeces-whose-body-will-one-day-be-the-culinary-delight-of-terrestrial-worms!"[7]   Less profanely and more eloquently, West notes that to be individuals is to be human and to be human,

---

6. Mendieta, "'What It Means to Be Human!'" 147.

7. West, *Sketches of My Culture.*

at the most profound level, is to encounter honestly the inescapable circumstances that constrain us, yet muster the courage to struggle compassionately for our own unique individualities and for more democratic and free societies. This courage contains the seeds of lived history—of memory, maturity, and melioration—in the face of no guaranteed harvest. Hence, my view of what it means to be human is preeminently existential—a focus on particular, singular, flesh-and-blood persons grappling with dire issues of death, dread, despair, disease and disappointment.[8]

To be human, however, is not merely a plight clothed in existential attire. To be human also means having the courage to take on life's challenges. This courage, West is careful to note, comes from his Chekhovian Christian sensibility, which "puts a premium on death and courage."[9] West's Chekhovian Christianity affords him the courage to look in the face of death, disease, and despair and still be hopeful. The question, "What does it mean to be modern?" speaks to our innate capacity to invoke change. West notes that to be modern has a good side and a bad one. The good side is an inherited endowment of rationality. The bad side is the enlightenment's systemic racism. West explains:

> My conception of what it means to be modern is shot through with a sense of the dialogical—the free encounter of mind, soul, and body that relates to others in order to be unsettled, unnerved and unhoused. This experience of dialogue—the I-Thou relation with the uncontrolled other—may result in a dizziness, vertigo or shudder that unhinges us from our moorings or yanks us from our anchors. This thoroughly modern lightness of being—produced, in part, from the innovations of modern science and technology or improvisations of modern music and the arts—is both frightening and energizing.[10]

Being modern leverages reason as an inherited asset to confront racist ideologies. Moreover, West's Chekhovian conception of "what it means to be modern" affords him the opportunity to:

> highlight the forms of self-making and self-creating of those whose suffering is often rendered invisible by the Enlightenment

8. West, *Cornel West Reader*, xvi–xvii.

9. West, *Cornel West Reader*, xvi.

10. West, *Cornel West Reader*, xviii–xix.

discourse on the light of natural reason and the Romantic preoccupation with imaginative transformation.[11]

To be sure, imagination creates resources that occasion transcendence beyond this place of terror and tears. Transformation looms despite horror and horrible predicaments and the mind's power to create empowering possibilities abounds.

The final question of practical importance, "What does it mean to be American?" transitions to a more theoretical aspect of West's vision of reality. To be American means involvement in democratic experiment. Which is to say that being American "is to be a part of a dialogical and democratic operation that grapples with the challenge of being human in an open-ended and experimental manner."[12] This experiment is a fragile endeavor, because it may force citizens to question certain modes of being that are tied to the American ethos. Yet for West it is a necessary experiment, because this experiment, democratic at its core, takes into consideration the needs of the most vulnerable in society. It is a worthy experiment, indeed. And, to be American is to open up vistas of possibilities. Even in the face of domestic terrors like slavery and failed democratic experiments, West still has hope:

> Have we reached the limits of the American religion of possibility? Do class, race, and gender hierarchy have the last word on how far democracy can go in our time? My Chekhovian Christian viewpoint says No! No! No![13]

Asking and answering these questions requires serious existential analysis, coupled with pragmatic perspectives. Yes, West's conception of reality is one that is fanned and fueled by the reality of death, disease, and despair. Yet these realities do not have the final say. It is important to note that although West's metaphysics has an existential component, it is not entirely existential. Improvisation facilitates maneuvering in search for meaningful ways to exist. West finds allies in American pragmatism as well as Afro-American critical thought. To the former, Lewis Gordon rhetorically quips that West is either a pragmatic existentialist or existential pragmatist. Though with an improvisational metaphysic, both theoretical trajectories work. Gordon,

---

11. West, *Cornel West Reader*, xviii.

12. West, *Cornel West Reader*, xviii.

13. West, *Cornel West Reader*, xx.

however, leans more toward the former, thereby downplaying pragmatism in favor of existentialism. Gordon makes the following observation:

> The odd thing is that when one actually reads West's sources of valuative inspiration, they are hardly pragmatic ones. Like that of Richard Rorty, who exercised much influence on his ideas, West's inspiration is patently existential. Rorty, however, wants to be so American that he fails to see the implications of wedding a European philosopher like Heidegger to John Dewey and working through a European literary figure like Nabokov to establish his claims. . . . Readers of Rorty should try, for a moment, to read Richard Rorty's recent *Philosophy and Social Hope* from an existential perspective and ask themselves why recent pragmatism seems to look more like existentialism than pragmatism. The power and consistency of West's thought is that he has been aware of the existential roots of his project from his early works onward.[14]

A nod to Gordon's point comes with trepidation. To say that Rorty and West are more existential than pragmatic unnecessarily overstates the case here. Why the dichotomy? To be sure, West clearly embraces existential notions like nihilism, freedom, and tragedy. His life experiences demand acquiescence. As a descendant of enslaved Africans, encounter with death and loss (of his own father), disease and despair shape his thinking. However, there is no real need to exaggerate the existential. The existential does not replace pragmatism but is the practical stage on which theory emerges. To this end, radical democracy as an offspring of existential democracy theorizes discursive means of discourse. With this, we turn to the influence John Dewey and Richard Rorty had on Cornel West's theoretical vision of reality, which involves notions of "radical democracy" and "individuality."

To the latter, which is Afro-American critical thought, is the theoretical outcome of West's version of prophetic Christianity, of which radical democracy and individuality are moral norms and from which West provides a genealogy of modern racism. Radical democracy and individuality, though moral norms of prophetic Christianity, are foundational for a postmodern ethic of radical freedom. Likewise, West's genealogy of modern racism is foundational because it exposes the rendering of vulnerable people, especially Black people, as victims of discourse. Anti-Black racism makes Black people subjects, yet this genealogy empowers through enlightenment, setting the conditions for flourishing.

14. Gordon, "Unacknowledged Fourth Tradition," 41.

Improvisation Continues: Genealogy, Radical Democracy, and Individuality

Practical recollection accounts for the value and virtue of my childhood experiences, spellbound by the seductive preaching of my paternal grandfather and maternal great-grandmother. Their examples embody a positive outlook and posture that occasioned transcendence beyond this place of wrath and tears. Unlike the members of Avondale Church of Christ who bought and sold a version of truth that damages, these preachers offered wholesale self-capitulation. They are case studies demonstrating the effectiveness and efficacy of prophetic Christianity this chapter explores. They articulated their story for themselves and used the pulpit as pedagogical platforms to retell racism's distorted narrative. Moreover, they exercised their agency as individuals and despite pigmentation that precludes privilege, they made sure their voices mattered. Without knowing the words, Rev. Fred Wesley and Moma Queen Esther Johnson were genealogical geniuses and were the exemplars of radical democracy and individuality.

Theoretically speaking, Cornel West offers two broad conceptual constructs, namely Afro-American critical thought and prophetic pragmatism. Both of these constructs contain the particular metaphysical conceptions, namely West's genealogical approach to understanding racism, and his vision of both radical democracy and individuality. As a genealogist, West explores alternative interpretations to dominant discourses in order to reenvision history. His methodology in *The American Evasion of Philosophy* comes out in the subtitle, *A Genealogy of American Pragmatism*. Thus, genealogy is an improvisational asset to addressing narratives that disempower vulnerable people. Radical democracy and individuality result from the direct influences of philosophers John Dewey and Richard Rorty on West's early intellectual and philosophical development. To this extent, an understanding of Dewey's metaphysics/naturalism and Rorty's metaphysics/anti-representationalism will deepen our appreciation of Cornel West's metaphysical norms. Specifically I show how John Dewey's naturalism influences Cornel West's metaphysics of radical democracy, individuality, and Richard Rorty's anti-representationalism on Cornel West's genealogy. The latter is a method of reconceptualizing and grappling with anti-Black racism and by extension pervasive xenophobia. All of these theoretical trajectories provide foundational tools for a postmodern ethic of radical freedom.

Racial genealogy, individuality, and radical democracy all fall under two theoretical concepts, Afro-American critical thought and prophetic pragmatism. Afro-American critical thought comes out of West's first major and comprehensive religious text, *Prophesy Deliverance: An Afro-American Revolutionary Christianity*. In this text, West puts forth his genealogy of modern racism and also makes a case for individuality and radical democracy being moral norms for prophetic Christian thought.[15] Along with American pragmatism, prophetic Christian thought serves as a source for Afro-American critical thought. Prophetic pragmatism comes out of *The American Evasion of Philosophy*, which is a formidable reconstruction of American pragmatism. This reconstruction entails a political interpretation of pragmatism and continues the discourse he begins in *Prophesy Deliverance*, making an even stronger case for individuality and radical democracy.

West's Genealogy of Modern Racism: Anti-Black Racism and Objectification

Chapter 2 of *Prophesy Deliverance* has the title, "A Genealogy of Modern Racism," and in this chapter West highlights the pervasiveness of white supremacy and the proliferation of pejorative racial depictions and objectifications of African Americans. Like Nietzsche and Foucault, West argues that our conceptions about truth, virtue, and aesthetics are social constructions. Moreover, Western conceptions of Black people come from the Blackness that whiteness created. By providing a genealogy of modern racism, West tells an alternative story to race construction. Giving his rationale for using this method, West explains the way his genealogy works:

> I call this inquiry a "genealogy" because following the works of Friedrich Nietzsche and Michel Foucault, I am interested in the emergence (Ensteburg) or the "moment of arising" of the idea of white supremacy within the modern discourse in the West. This genealogy tries to address the following questions: What are the discursive conditions for the possibility of the intelligibility and legitimacy of the idea of white supremacy in modern discourse? How is this idea constituted within the epistemological field of

15. It is helpful to add that West uses Afro-American critical thought and Afro-American religious thought interchangeably. He notes that prophetic Christianity is a source for Afro-American critical/religious thought for which radical democracy and individuality serve as moral norms.

> modern discourse? What is the complex configuration of meta-phors, notions, categories, and norms which produced and promoted such an object of modern discourse?[16]

The questions raised in this quotation are foundational for West's genealogy, because answering them exposes the deep-seated biased assumptions about reality, particularly white supremacy, and highlights the kind of language used in modern discourse to perpetuate white supremacy.

Through his genealogical method, West argues that racial categories and depictions are critical for modernity because these categories and depictions legitimize the discourses on race, especially the white race. Another way to say this is that modernity employed science and rational proofs to promote anti-Black racism. At the practical level, these racist sentiments seemed empirical and therefore true. Once these notions take root in collective consciousness, for white as well as Black people, unrooting will take decades, if not years.

As West notes in the quotation above, the structure of modern racism comes with dominant conceptions about Blackness, and the proliferation and perpetuation of these concepts relied on controlling metaphors, notions, categories, and norms.[17] Some of the controlling metaphors include the devaluing of Blackness. Or that Blackness symbolizes evil or limited moral capability. This is also the case with notions and categories that demeaned Black beauty, intelligence, and even rendered Black people as less than human. Controlling norms determine interactions and reactions to Black people especially in light of the established metaphors, notions, and categories.

For West, three historical processes determine these metaphors, notions, categories, and norms: the scientific revolution, the Cartesian transformation of philosophy, and the classical revival.[18] The scientific revolution occasioned "new modes of knowledge and new conceptions of truth and reality,"[19] thereby giving science authority to mitigate between false and true reality. This authority to mitigate reality confirms and validates already established perceptions about Blackness.[20] The Cartesian transformation of philosophy gave primacy to the subject and preeminence to

16. West, *Prophesy Deliverance*, 48.

17. West, *Prophesy Deliverance*, 50.

18. West, *Prophesy Deliverance*, 50.

19. West, *Prophesy Deliverance*, 51.

20. West, *Prophesy Deliverance*, 51.

representation.[21] Primacy to the subject simply means that even without empirical experience, the thinking subject (in this case white people) can trust intuitions about Blackness. For Descartes, the senses deceive you and therefore, it's suspect to rely on experience.[22] The classical revival takes place during the Renaissance and promoted humanist studies and Latin literature. This promotion gave value to certain forms of art and literature, thereby placing value on certain types of aesthetic forms. West highlights these forms that are concomitant with the classical revival, because they infuse "Greek ocular metaphors and classical ideas of beauty, proportion, and moderation into the beginnings of modern discourse."[23]

By pointing out the developments in science, philosophy, art, and literature, West reveals the logic endemic in the structure of modernity and shows how discourse rendered Black people inferior. In his genealogy, West shows that modern discourse on race begins with making connections between skin color and beauty, morality, and intelligence. These connections indicate logic so deep within the Western psyche that their truth is taken for granted. This logic will "produce and prohibit, develop and delimit, specific conceptions of truth and knowledge, beauty and character, so that certain ideals are rendered incomprehensible and unintelligible."[24]

Even Western philosophers like Immanuel Kant, David Hume, and Thomas Jefferson theorized that Black people lacked sound reasoning and astute moral judgment. These philosophers rendered Black people intellectually, morally, and aesthetically inferior. Such rationale become reified in academic and scientific communities. And given that the academy is a venue that disseminates information about culture, class, race, ethics, etc., it is not surprising that racial categories and depictions seemed objective during the enlightenment.[25]

This genealogy exposes the "discursive conditions for the possibility of the intelligibility and legitimacy of white supremacy in modern discourse?"[26] These discursive conditions produce anti-Blackness as well as what West calls, "the secretions of white supremacy."[27] These discursive conditions

---

21. West, *Prophesy Deliverance*, 52.

22. West, *Prophesy Deliverance*, 52.

23. West, *Prophesy Deliverance*, 53.

24. West, *Prophesy Deliverance*, 48.

25. West, *Prophesy Deliverance*, 61–62.

26. West, *Prophesy Deliverance*, 48.

27. West, *Prophesy Deliverance*, 48.

come from pervasive and prevailing theories and superstructures formed in modernity. West argues that structures of modern discourse produce forms of rationality, scientificity, and objectivity as well as construct cultural and aesthetic ideals. These structures lay dormant, as it were, beneath the domain of discourse, making it easy to escape ordinary consciousness.

West is careful to distinguish his genealogy from Marxist analysis of power. Genealogy differs from the Marxist's analysis of superstructure in that his analysis fails to make the connection between forms of economic production and the power that is immanent within nondiscursive structures. In his own words, West announces the following:

> I am further suggesting that there is no direct correspondence between nondiscursive structures, such as a system of production (or, in Marxist terms, an economic base), and discursive structures, such as theoretical formations (or, in Marxist terms, an ideological superstructure). Rather, there are powers immanent in nondiscursive structures and discursive structures.[28]

West unveils that Black people are rendered inferior at both the discursive and nondiscursive levels, suggesting that it is both theory (discursive) and practice (nondiscursive) that inform modern discourse. Given that West's genealogy subscribes immanent power at both levels, he is suggesting that power is the key ingredient in the proliferation of pejorative perceptions of Black people, further bolstering the point that white supremacy seems scientific and objective. Given the tenets of modern discourse, the proliferation of white supremacy, and the presumptions of the objectivity of Black inferiority, the need is to utilize a metaphysical outlook that corrects the pejorative conceptions, enhances Black life, and empowers African Americans to change their predicament. I think that West's conceptions of individuality and radical democracy are steps in the right direction. To these metaphysical items we now turn.

Rorty and Dewey: Historical Antecedents to Individuality and Radical Democracy

Richard Rorty's anti-representationalism and John Dewey's naturalism are philosophical antecedents to West's metaphysics of radical democracy and individualism. Rorty's views on anti-representationalism and his

28. West, *Prophesy Deliverance*, 48.

disagreements with conceptions of objectivity influence West's affirmation of the individual within community and the negation of objectivity. Dewey's naturalism influences West's conception of reality as well as West's conception of radical democracy. The following discusses both philosophers' positions, then connects the dots to West's own version of reality.

Rorty: What's in Here May Not Be What's Out There

Noted much earlier in this book is that the analytic philosophical position that the mind can represent reality. This representationalist perspective partly underscores the philosophy of language's position, that only language accurately represents the world "out there."[29] Rorty rejects that people are able "to pick and choose among the contents of our minds or our language and say this or that item 'corresponds to' or 'represents' the environment in a way that some other does not."[30]

Historical precedence for this is Descartes' belief that the mind can know indubitably and with certainty what's out there in the world. In other words, ideas in the mind accurately represent reality. Rorty disagrees. He argues that it is our experiences that determine how we understand reality and the world and affirm that the mind apprehends only mental representations of material objects. But the mind does not apprehend the objects themselves.[31] This is a metaphysical position indeed and one that denies a reality independent of the mind. In other words, a world "out there" is a result of how we experience and live in it.[32] Put more theoretically, Rorty states:

> Indeed, he or she insists on this point—that our minds or our language could not (as the representationalist skeptic fears) be "out of touch with the reality" any more than our bodies could. What he or she denies is that it is explanatorily useful to pick and choose among the contents of our minds or our language and say that this

29. For further reading on the representationalist/anti-representationalist debate, see McGinn, "Radical Interpretation and Epistemology"; Dummett, *Truth and Other Enigmas*; Davidson, *Inquiries into Truth*.

30. Rorty, *Objectivity, Relativism, and Truth*, 5.

31. Rorty, *Objectivity, Relativism, and Truth*, 5.

32. Rorty, *Objectivity, Relativism, and Truth*, 5.

> or that item "corresponds to" or "represents" the environment in a way that some other item does not.[33]

Our experiences determine what the world looks like for us. Rorty concedes that we color our own apprehension of reality, but that does not undermine the credibility of experience.

Deeper insight on Rorty's position is debated with Thomas Nagel's position on representationalism. This debate is in the article "Richard Rorty and the Radical Left," by legal expert William G. Weaver. The article discusses how Rorty rejects notions of objectivity, convergence, and privileged discourse. Like the proponents of objectivity noted earlier, Nagel also believes that there is a reality independent of experience and espouses that we should not taint reality by our experiences. To the contrary, Rorty asserts that experience is the only way to account for reality.[34]

To further argue for objectivity, Nagel asserts the reality of "things in themselves," which distinguishes between "the real" and our perception of "the real." Nagel contends for these "things in themselves and that we should not rely on the specifics of one's individual makeup."[35] Nagel further contends that "the further we can carry our thoughts from the particular, concrete events of our lives, the closer we come to an overarching truth about classes of events or the world in which those events occur."[36] Rorty disagrees and warns that thinking of reality objectively comes at a great cost to concrete experiences. And as Weaver points out, "Rorty thinks we should skip the talk about universals and concentrate on multiplying the particulars."[37] This leads to Rorty's more constructive solution, which is his notion of solidarity.

Rorty's notion of solidarity celebrates both the concreteness and the specificity of our social and historical contexts, thereby suggesting that consent for what is real in a particular social and historical context comes from intersubjective agreement.[38] For Rorty, intersubjective agreement means listening more carefully to those who are suffering and who may come with

---

33. Rorty, *Objectivity, Relativism, and Truth*, 5.
34. Rorty, *Objectivity, Relativism, and Truth*, 731.
35. Rorty, *Objectivity, Relativism, and Truth*, 734.
36. Rorty, *Objectivity, Relativism, and Truth*, 734.
37. Rorty, *Objectivity, Relativism, and Truth*, 735.
38. Rorty, *Objectivity, Relativism, and Truth*, 12.

new ideas.[39] Solidarity means listening to, although not always agreeing with, others outside of our particular and local context. Rorty notes:

> There are two principal ways in which reflective human beings try, by placing lives in a larger context, to give sense to those lives. The first is by telling the story of their contribution to a community. This community may be the actual historical one in which they live, or another actual one, distant in time or place or a quite imaginary one, consisting perhaps of a dozen heroes and heroines selected from history or fiction or both. The second way is to describe themselves as standing in immediate relation to a nonhuman reality. This relation is immediate in the sense that it does not derive from a relation between such a reality and their tribe, or their nation, or their imagined band of comrades. I shall say that stories of the former kind exemplify the desire for solidarity, and that stories of the latter kind exemplify the desire for objectivity. Insofar as she seeks objectivity, she distances herself from the actual persons around her not by thinking of herself as a member of some other real or imaginary group, but rather by attaching herself to something which can be described without reference to any particular human beings.[40]

Rorty's beautiful quotation here is clear. Individuals who seek for objectivity may potentially engage themselves in a fictive or irrelevant reality that has little if anything to do with their concrete experiences. Moreover, by seeking out objectivity, they estrange themselves from their particular reality and may even negate the value of their own reality.[41]

Here is where individuality has critical importance for Rorty, and subsequently, for West. Rorty's position on solidarity highlights the importance of the individual within community, and his anti-representationalism safeguards individuals from trying to embrace a metaphysical outlook that damages well-being. West runs with this metaphysical outlook and carries it to its pragmatic end. Objectivity and turning people into objects potentially wombs the well-being, and the value of theories like anti-representationalism and solidarity is they affirm individuality and concrete and unique experiences. Thanks to Rorty, West now adds to his improvisational repertoire a metaphysic that affirms and empowers. And for a postmodern ethic

---

39. Rorty, *Objectivity, Relativism, and Truth*, 12–13.

40. Rorty, *Objectivity, Relativism, and Truth*, 21.

41. For a good case made against Rorty's notion of solidarity, see: Amesbury, *Morality and Social Criticism.*

of radical freedom, to affirm individuality empowers African Americans and vulnerable people to change the way they see themselves and perhaps the way others see them.

Individuality exalts selfhood, whereas notions of objective reality may render some inferior to others. Protracted pejorative notions of race, gender, and sex come from the historical proliferation of presumptuous truth claims regarding these notions. West advocates for individualism, which presumes that what is good, beautiful, etc., must never have basis in some authorized objective standard. Therefore, an ethic of radical freedom uses West's improvisational metaphysic of individuality as a foundational asset.

Dewey: Anti-Metaphysics, Metaphysics, Naturalism, and Existential Democracy

This sections makes the case for Dewey's direct influence on Cornel West's metaphysics, first, disclosing that both men reject metaphysics for good and for the same reason. The second case is an extension of the first case. That is, Dewey's naturalism is his metaphysics for the same reason that radical democracy is a component of Cornel West's metaphysics. The third case differs from the first two in that Dewey's creative democracy influences West's radical democracy, yet there are some differences, most importantly Dewey's failure to incorporate the tragic within his work.

A couple of years ago I had the privilege of a conversation with an African American philosopher who specializes in Cornel West and John Dewey, and he contends that reading West theoretically is reading Dewey theoretically. When I pointed out obvious differences especially regarding discussions about race, tragedy, the blues, hip hop, etc., he retorted that these are mere applications of West's theoretical work. After spending considerable time reading Dewey, I certainly see his point, though there are critical diverging points between them. Those points, notwithstanding and later discussed, I now focus on one similarity that undeniably shows Dewey's influence on West. Already noted is Dewey's naturalism on West's thought, but one critical similarity is worth noting. That is, the philosophical correctness of even asserting that Dewey or West are doing metaphysics at all. In fact, some scholarship contends that Dewey's naturalism is anti-metaphysical. Arguably, West's critique of metaphysics signals an absence of anything metaphysical. Obviously I disagree with the latter of these positions. Moreover, I concomitantly disagree that Dewey has a metaphysical agenda for the reason I believe West has one. Paradoxically, their rejection of traditional metaphysics is the grounds for their metaphysics, namely, an anti-metaphysics metaphysics.

Without much ado, the parallel argument is that both West and Dewey believe that experience is the locus for what's real, and the problem with traditional metaphysics is its focus on the transcendental, absolute, and the supernatural to determine what's real. This doesn't mean that neither philosopher denies the existence of these notions. West is a Christian who time and time again acknowledges belief in the Absolute, and in fact, is a lay Baptist preacher. Similarly, though Dewey rejects organized religion and belief in a supernatural being, he does, at least implicitly, value a religious attitude in education and pedagogy. In "My Pedagogic Creed," he avows that a teacher "always is the prophet of the true God and the ushered in of the true kingdom of God."[42]

John Dewey's naturalism also influences West's notion of individuality and radical democracy. Dewey's naturalism accents the importance of social, existential, and cultural backgrounds of people's experiences. As his seminal text shows, Dewey accents the value of nature, that is, generic traits of all of humanity. One such trait is the dignity of all humanity regardless of race, gender, national origin, and so on. He also values experience in that our vision of the world dictates our responses. Our culture informs our experience and our experience informs our culture. To this end, Dewey values the educational process as instrumental in seeking solutions to existential misfortunes, improving culture, and advancing a future of egalitarian equality.[43]

Dewey's influence reveals that metaphysical discourse involves cultural concerns. In his book *Consequences of Pragmatism*, Richard Rorty makes a case that Dewey's naturalism accents the social, existential, and cultural influences of Dewey's metaphysics. In chapter 5 of *Consequences of Pragmatism*, titled "Dewey's Metaphysics," Rorty argues that Dewey's metaphysics seem more like a philosophy of culture. In fact, on page 72 of the essay, Rorty suggests that Dewey's principal metaphysical text, *Nature and Experience*, could easily be changed to *Nature and Culture*,[44] primarily because Dewey understands human experiences to be a product of culture. "Dewey's book," Rorty points out, "consists, very roughly, of accounts

42. Dewey, "My Pedagogic Creed," 95.
43. Dewey, *Democracy and Education*.
44. Rorty, *Consequences of Pragmatism*, 72.

of the historic and cultural genesis of the problems traditionally dubbed 'metaphysical.'"[45]

Harvard philosopher Peter Godfrey-Smith seems to agree with Rorty and makes the argument as well that Dewey's naturalism is akin to a discourse on culture and its problems. In an essay entitled "Dewey on Naturalism, Realism and Science," Godfrey-Smith argues that Dewey's naturalism must be understood "from within a framework provided by our best current scientific description of human beings and their relations to their environments."[46]

Dewey notes in an essay entitled "Half-Hearted Naturalism" that his brand of metaphysics concerns itself with the world in which humankind lives and how this world is comprised of suffering, enjoyment, success, etc:

> This is the extent and method of my "metaphysics": the large and constant features of human sufferings, enjoyments, trials, failures, and successes together with the institutions of art, science, technology, politics, and religion which mark them, communicate genuine features of the world within which man lives. The method differs no whit from that of any investigator who, by making certain observations and experiments, and by utilizing the existing body of ideas available for calculation and interpretation concludes that he really succeeds in finding out something about some limited aspect of nature. If there is any novelty in Experience and Nature, it is not, I should say, this "metaphysics," which is that of the common man but lies in the use made of the method to understand a group of special problems which have troubled philosophy.[47]

This quotation clearly indicates Dewey's concerns for the human predicament and the cultural and intellectual resources available to assist humankind to engage human sufferings, enjoyments, trials, failures, and successes. Dewey thinks that intellectual discourse and particularly philosophy must be about the business of solving human problems. For this reason, Dewey considers the philosophy of his time to be pseudo-problems in philosophy,[48]

---

45. Rorty, *Consequences of Pragmatism*, 72.

46. Godfrey-Smith, "Dewey on Naturalism," 25–35. For further reading by Godfrey-Smith on Dewey's naturalism see Godfrey-Smith, "Dewey and the Question of Realism."

47. Dewey, "Half-Hearted Naturalism," 59. For further discussion, see Dewey, *Experience and Nature*.

48. Dewey, "Half-Hearted Naturalism," 59.

while, as far as he is concerned, the real philosophical problems take into consideration social, political, and existential realities.[49]

Although Cornel West hardly (if ever) refers to naturalism in his writings, he does make reference both to Dewey's anti-realism and his bent toward historicism. As discussed in the previous chapter, both anti-realism and historicism are critical to West's epistemology. However, although they are not critical to West's metaphysics, Dewey's naturalism presents a version of reality that lacks objectivity and dogmatism.[50] Like Dewey, West situates his pragmatism in the context of cultural and social concerns and these concerns make philosophical discourse relevant and important. In fact, West sees pragmatism coming into maturation through the work of Dewey. West bases this on the fact that Dewey, more than his pragmatic predecessors, brought direct attention to the social and political arena. Like Dewey, West's prophetic pragmatism seeks to bring amelioration to the pain of vulnerable people. To this extent, West presents his prophetic pragmatism as a form of "future-oriented instrumentalism that tries to deploy thought as a weapon to enable more effective action."[51]

Although scholars do not make a connection with West's prophetic pragmatism and metaphysics, M. Shawn Copeland and Hilary Putnam situate prophetic pragmatism in the context of democratic and existential concerns. In her essay "Cornel West's Improvisational Philosophy of Religion," Copeland assesses West's prophetic Christian thought and argues that West's philosophical reasoning centers on answering existential and ontological questions. In the following quotation she reveals the influence of Dewey as well as summarizes West's philosophical project:

> His project calls for a renascence of philosophizing in the tradition of John Dewey. . . . And whether that tradition may be tainted with anti-Platonism, West's concerns are redolent of that far, far older tradition of philosophy which insists that the most important problem of philosophy is the problem of the right way, the most choice worthy way, to live.[52]

Hilary Putnam also makes the case that Dewey's pragmatism influences West's conception of creative democracy. In his essay "Pragmatism Resurgent: A Reading of *The American Evasion of Philosophy*," Putnam states:

49. Rorty, *Consequences of Pragmatism*, 75.
50. West, *American Evasion of Philosophy*, 88–89.
51. West, *American Evasion of Philosophy*, 5.
52. Copeland, "Cornel West's Improvisational Philosophy," 154–55.

> Again like West, Dewey valued democracy while refusing to shut his eyes to the distance we have to travel if we are to achieve real democracy. For real democracy, Dewey consistently taught, is not just a matter of counting votes; it is the ideal of real participation in the decision-making process by those affected by the decisions to be made, it requires a new kind of education, a new way of applying intelligence to social problems, and what he called a "democratic faith," an attitude toward individuals that manifests itself in all of one's personal relations and not just in "public life." In addition, the centrality of aesthetic experience to what we may call, Dewey's "philosophical anthropology" is obvious.[53]

For West as for Dewey, an individual's voice in the way life is governed is of critical importance, and also for West, the remedy to social problems is the application of "radical democratic faith." Indeed, Victor Anderson's claim that the Christian faith, for West, is reducible to "radical democracy" makes even more sense, just as West's argument is logical that a metaphysic of radical democracy and individuality entails ontological and existential concerns.

As stated above, West's metaphysical conception of individuality and radical democracy takes shape in his major religious text, *Prophesy Deliverance*, and his major philosophical text, *American Evasion of Philosophy*. In *Prophesy Deliverance*, West puts forth a theory of Afro-American critical thought, where individuality and radical democracy are moral norms for prophetic Christianity and Afro-American critical thought, respectively. In *American Evasion of Philosophy*, West puts forth his theory of prophetic pragmatism where individuality and radical democracy are embodied in three Emersonian tropes, namely, power, provocation, and personality. The rest of this chapter is an in-depth exploration of these Westian theories and their elucidation of the metaphysics of individuality and radical democracy.

Individuality and Radical Democracy as Presented in *Prophesy Deliverance*

In the introduction of *Prophesy Deliverance*, West notes that democracy and individuality are moral norms of prophetic Christianity and these norms are the critical ingredients for positively changing the lives of African Americans. Prophetic Christianity provides a catalyst for this change,

53. Putnam, "Pragmatism Resurgent," 24–25. For additional discussion of Putnam's assessment on Dewey, see Putnam and Putnam "Education for Democracy"; Putnam, "Reconsideration of Deweyan Democracy."

resulting in what West hopes to be a revolutionary Christianity that will replace priestly forms of Christianity as well as sidestep the pitfalls of epistemic foundations and objective truths. West presents a brilliant argument for why such a revolutionary Christianity is necessary and also makes a case for the norms of which it will consist. A revolutionary Christianity must take into consideration the plight of ordinary people, especially African Americans, and create effective ways to deal with the social maladies of racism, sexism, and oppression. His theological reference point is Black liberation theology, showing how it may be enhanced and improved. Liberation will come through radical democracy and individuality.[54] These norms espouse the principle of self-realization, where individuals find meaning within community.

This principle entails three critical notions. The first is the understanding that every individual "regardless of class, country, cast, race, or sex should have opportunity to fulfill his or her potentialities."[55] The second is the dignity of persons and depravity of persons. This notion illuminates how human nature is endowed with a capacity to resolve problems and to inflict pain. The third notion is the dialectic of contradiction and transformation. Contradiction presupposes what presently is and transformation implies the ability to change the prevailing reality.[56]

Radical democracy reflects the depravity of persons and the dignity of persons. It reflects the depravity of persons in that it acknowledges that human beings are imperfect and prone to selfishness and self-centeredness. And given that we are imperfect, we are capable of exercising injustice and inhumanity. It reflects the dignity of persons in that it accents the fact that human persons are able to change their realities. That is, regardless of our circumstances in life, radical democracy gives voice to every person despite his or her social and political status.

That radical democracy and individuality are norms of prophetic Christianity is an expression of a dialectic of human nature and human history. This dialectic of human history and human nature is the amalgam of four sub-dialectics. The first is a dialectic of imperfect products and transformative practice, the second is a dialectic of prevailing realities

---

54. West is careful to point out that the individuality integral to his project is not the same as "doctrinaire individualism," which views persons as "maximizers of pleasure and appropriators of unlimited resources." See West, *Prophesy Deliverance*, 16.

55. West, *Prophesy Deliverance*, 16.

56. West, *Prophesy Deliverance*, 17.

and negation, the third is a dialectic of human depravity and human dignity, and the fourth dialectic is a dialectic of "what is" and "the not yet."[57] The dialectic of human history and human nature essentially notes that although history bears witness to the depravity of human nature and its proclivity to cause harm and destruction, the very nature of individuals is such that they are able to change their circumstances from "what is" to "what ought to be."[58]

This dialectic of human nature and human history presents the ontological and existential realities that preclude human flourishing; yet it unveils the intrinsic power of individuals to confront these realities and threats. Ontologically, this dialectic affirms the dignity of all human beings while also recognizing these threats and is quite aware of humankind's proclivity to evoke pain. Both individuality and democracy are ways to ensure that the citizens most vulnerable to threats of nonbeing have a voice in the way their lives are governed. Therefore, democracy and individuality are collateral resources to ensure that vulnerable people can combat threats to nonbeing.

The reality of the dignity of persons and the depravity of persons resembles Reinhold Niebuhr's insistence on the need for democracy. Niebuhr states it very well when he declares: "man's inclination for justice makes democracy possible. Man's capacity for injustice makes democracy necessary."[59] Humankind's proclivity to be selfish, oppressive, and destructive to others makes democracy necessary for ensuring freedom and liberation to the most vulnerable in society. These metaphysical assumptions ensure more promising possibilities in that human beings are capable of transforming current realities. West invokes the power imbued within human beings to exude metaphysical possibilities and to transcend the ontological threat of nonbeing.

From an existential perspective, although death, disease, and despair are inevitable, the dialectic of human history and human nature ushers in existential and social freedom. Existential freedom is the human proclivity to release oneself from bondage to death, disease, and despair:

> The basic contribution of prophetic Christianity, despite the countless calamities perpetrated by Christian churches, is that

57. West, *Prophesy Deliverance*, 17.

58. West, *Prophesy Deliverance*, 17.

59. Niebuhr, *Children of Light*.

every individual regardless of class, country, caste, race, or sex should have the opportunity to fulfill his or her potentialities.[60]

As is the case with Rorty's anti-representationalism and Dewey's naturalism, of critical importance for West is a metaphysic of cultural products, resources, and influences. Individuals come out of communities that shape their outlook on life and reality. In this way, their reality is their reality, and unbeknownst to them they have the power to contribute to the unfolding of normative discourse. Oftentimes, displaced people within communities employ this power. Because of their dignity, they possess the power to initiate change. In other words, through their dignity as individuals, they possess the power to transform "what is" into "what ought to be."

In chapter 4 of *Prophesy Deliverance*, West brings prophetic Christian thought into a dialogical relationship with progressive Marxism. He does this hoping to "demystify the deep misunderstanding and often outright ignorance each side has of the other."[61] Like prophetic Christian thought, progressive Marxism relies on the metaphysical assumption that "what is" can be transformed to "what ought to be." However, instead of a dialectic of human nature and human dignity (prophetic Christianity) Marxism promotes a dialectic of human practice and human nature. Like Christianity, it embraces a view of human nature, but that human nature collapses in human practice under the conditions of history.

> This collapse of human nature into human practice and into human history—as opposed to a dialectical relation of human practice and to human history—is the distinctive difference Christianity and Marxism.[62]

For prophetic Christianity, the Marxist dialectic of human nature and human practice is a bit too optimistic, primarily because history has not been all that good to African Americans. West is willing to concede, however, that the one important thing prophetic Christianity can gain from a Marxist dialectic is a critique of capitalist structures and regimes, especially when those regimes perpetuate economic oppression.

60. West, *Prophesy Deliverance*, 16.

61. West, *Prophesy Deliverance*, 23.

62. West, *Prophesy Deliverance*, 19.

Individuality and Radical Democracy as Presented in *The American Evasion of Philosophy*

Like Afro-American critical thought, prophetic pragmatism depends on the norms of individuality and radical democracy, and these norms are elucidated in *The American Evasion of Philosophy*. The power individuals possess is to transform their realities from "what is" to "what ought to be," and both *The American Evasion of Philosophy* and *Prophesy Deliverance* are resources to make that transformation. These sources contain radical democracy and individuality as moral norms; yet while West unpacks prophetic Christianity as a source in *Prophesy Deliverance*, he dedicates only five pages to a discussion of the relevance of American pragmatism as a source for Afro-American critical thought. I contend that *The American Evasion of Philosophy* answers the nagging question (at least nagging to me), "How is American pragmatism a source for Afro-American critical thought?" One way to answer that is to read *The American Evasion of Philosophy* as a continuation of the conversation West began in *Prophesy Deliverance* which, I argue, can be understood as his reconstruction of American pragmatism into prophetic pragmatism.

To make a case for prophetic pragmatism, West weaves various disciplines into one philosophical cloth so that *The American Evasion of Philosophy* may be best understood as a social history of ideas.[63] As a social history of ideas, *The American Evasion of Philosophy* "conceives of the intellectual sphere of history as distinct, unique, and personal sets of cultural practices intimately connected with concomitant developments in the larger society and culture."[64] Thus, philosophical discourse is no longer an abstract venue preoccupied with logical puzzles, language games, and epistemic certainty. Instead, West's prophetic pragmatism responds to oppression and social and political impediments. To carry out this agenda, West writes the text as a genealogy of American pragmatism in order to include a historian (W. E. B. Du Bois), a theologian (Reinhold Niebuhr), a sociologist (C. Wright Mills), and a literary critic (Lionel Trilling).[65]

In the introduction to *The American Evasion of Philosophy*, West explains why it is that pragmatism has experienced a recent resurgence. He offers three reasons. The first is the disenchantment with traditional

---

63. West, *American Evasion of Philosophy*, 6.

64. West, *American Evasion of Philosophy*, 6.

65. West, *American Evasion of Philosophy*, 6.

philosophy as a transcendental mode of inquiry, "a tribunal of reason which grounds claims about Truth, Goodness, and Beauty."[66] This is problematic because when philosophy is transcendental, philosophers determine both objective truth and objective reality, thus rendering the powerful more powerful and the vulnerable more vulnerable. Pragmatism argues that this mode of inquiry is unhelpful and "unwilling to move into the frightening wilderness of pragmatism and historicism with their concomitant concerns in social theory, cultural criticism, and historiography."[67] The second reason for this disenchantment has to do with the relationship between knowledge and power, cognition and control, discourse and politics.[68] This disenchantment highlights the problematic notion of correlating morality, art, and science with structures of domination and control. To counter this rationale requires pointing out that the currently pervasive forms of reasoning and scientific discovery are the products of social and historical constructs. The third reason for this disenchantment with traditional philosophy is its proclivity to objectify historical subjects rendering them inferior. Gone are the days when the elite ordained themselves as cultural creators who ignore social structural constraints and "constraints that reinforce and reproduce hierarchies based on class, race, gender, and sexual orientation."[69]

Given these three areas of disenchantment, West ascribes to pragmatism the capacity to reinvigorate "moribund academic life, our lethargic political life, our decadent cultural life, and our chaotic personal lives for the flowering of many-sided personalities and the flourishing of more democracy and freedom."[70] Thanks to Dewey and Rorty, philosophical discourse in general and metaphysics in particular present an understanding of reality that celebrates difference and accentuates the virtues of "the least of these."

From a metaphysical point of view, American pragmatism offers a view of the universe that gives individuals a variety of possibilities. Like Afro-American critical thought, pragmatism offers a liberal conception of the individual where she is not locked into an ontological category and confined to a certain existential space. Clevis Headley, in an essay entitled "Critical Evaluations of Prophetic Pragmatism," echoes this point regarding

66. West, *American Evasion of Philosophy*, 3.

67. West, *American Evasion of Philosophy*, 3.

68. West, *American Evasion of Philosophy*, 3.

69. West, *American Evasion of Philosophy*, 4.

70. West, *American Evasion of Philosophy*, 4.

this liberal conception of the individual and also argues that such an individual has limited possibilities:

> pragmatism shuns deterministic conceptions of the universe, and actively underscores the ineradicable presence of chance, contingency, and novelty as features of the universe. . . . Hence, pragmatism rejects metaphysical closure in the sense of holding that we can obtain some absolutist conception of the universe that is not limited by the temporal flux of things, a conception that answers determinately to some principle or concept. . . . And, finally pragmatism readily supports a radical pluralism. . . . Pragmatic pluralism celebrates the plurality of traditions, cultures, perspectives, cognitive schemes, and philosophical orientations.[71]

This quotation explicitly points to a conception of the universe that is dynamic; this quotation implicitly points to a conception of an individual who is a cultural and social substance. Although Headley references pragmatism in its broader conception, this quotation unveils Rorty's anti-representationalism and Dewey's naturalism, which ultimately influence West's metaphysical conception of individual and radical democracy.

West's version of pragmatism highlights individual virtues and value while at the same time creating a platform for the "least of these" to have a voice about the governing of their lives. Like others of his pragmatist constituency, West negates an epistemologically based philosophy. But unlike them, West evades epistemologically based philosophy by promoting power, provocation, and personality as manifestations of individuality and radical democracy.

Along with American pragmatism, *The American Evasion of Philosophy* acknowledges the need to evade epistemologically based philosophy while at the same time concerning itself with social analysis, democracy, and a preoccupation with unchecked power. Comparing American pragmatism with the methodology of analytic philosophy, West notes the efficacy of the former:

> It is no accident that American pragmatism once again rises to the surface of North Atlantic intellectual life at the present moment. For its major themes of evading epistemology-centered philosophy, accenting human powers, and transforming antiquated modes of social hierarchies in light of religious and/or ethical ideals make it relevant and attractive. The distinctive appeal of American

71. Headley, "Cornel West on Prophesy," 61–62.

pragmatism in our postmodern moment is its unashamedly moral emphasis and its unequivocally ameliorative impulse.[72]

It is this emphasis on "accenting human powers" and "transforming antiquated modes of social hierarchies" that gives West's prophetic pragmatism metaphysical and existential relevance. It has metaphysical relevance because prophetic pragmatism promotes a view of reality as malleable. By bequeathing to citizens the power to change their realities, it eschews social hierarchies that may preclude the decent quality of life for those who are most vulnerable. It has existential relevance inasmuch as it recognizes tragic realities in the lives of people, thereby seeking helpful ways to answer the questions implied in the human situation.

West does his constructive work relying heavily on Ralph Waldo Emerson's employment of power, provocation, and personality as tropes that give rise to radical democracy. These tropes energize individual impulses toward creating democratic ideals that ensure a better America. West notes that Emerson's "rhetorical strategies, [are] principally aimed at explaining America to itself."[73] This process of explaining America to itself entails weaving "novel notions of power, provocation, and personality into a potent and emerging American ideology of voluntaristic invulnerability and utopian possibility.[74]

Regarding power, Emerson held a metaphysical vision of a mythic self. This mythic self employs rhetoric as a way of transcending and transforming current realities and situations. Emerson understood power in three ways. First, power is multileveled in that "encompasses and distinguishes the powers of the nation, the economy, the person, tradition and language."[75] Second, Emerson celebrates the "expansion of . . . transgressive acts of the literate populace that promote moral aims and personal fulfillment."[76] And third, Emerson viewed power as a function forging dynamic relations within nature, showing the ever-emerging development of historical consciousness.[77]

Provocation, for Emerson, is a means by which one is able to critique existing social and economic structures. This critique entails examining

---

72. West, *American Evasion of Philosophy*, 4.

73. West, *American Evasion of Philosophy*, 10.

74. West, *American Evasion of Philosophy*, 10.

75. West, *American Evasion of Philosophy*, 10.

76. West, *American Evasion of Philosophy*, 10.

77. West, *American Evasion of Philosophy*, 10–11.

both the good and bad side of market culture and highlighting the weakness of capitalism. We learn from Emerson that we have the right to provoke prevailing and pervasive institutions that do harm to our well-being. For example, during the civil rights movement, vulnerable African American citizens had a right to provoke the pervasive notion of separate but equal.

West highlights the distinction between an early idealistic Emerson and a later realistic Emerson. The early Emerson vilified the proliferation of market culture because he believed this culture limited the development of a self that possessed dynamic possibilities. Preoccupation with the market directs one's attention to useless resources that do little for the soul of humankind. Later Emerson came to terms with the fact that market forces are integral to existence. In a more positive vein, Emerson "projects a conception of the self that can be easily appropriated by market culture for its own perpetuation and reproduction."[78]

Although his position on the cultural market changed, his view regarding capitalism remained constant. Emerson regarded the reification in capitalist exchange relations as yet another way to objectify and "thingify" persons. Hence, he concluded, the aim of provocation was "to subjectify and humanize unique individuals."[79] West views this subjectification and humanization of individuals to have both abstract and concrete ramifications:

> In the abstract, this ideal is antihierarchical, egalitarian, and democratic, for it pertains to personal relations. In the concrete, it virtually evaporates because it cannot but relate to marginal persons on the edges of dominant classes, groups, or elites. In this way, Emerson's view of a self that provokes and thrives on being provoked converges yet never fully coincides with the instrumental self engendered by market forces.[80]

This quotation speaks of an individuality that empowers all human beings and such empowerment opens up possibilities to interrogate structures of power and domination.

The third trope West describes is personality, which he sees as Emerson's conviction of the dignity and worth of human beings regardless of social and economic status in life. Paradoxically, the dignity and worth of all individuals does not mean that all are created equal. West attempts to nuance Emerson's racist perspectives with his abolitionist sensibilities. A

78. West, *American Evasion of Philosophy*, 27.

79. West, *American Evasion of Philosophy*, 27.

80. West, *American Evasion of Philosophy*, 27–28.

product of his time, Emerson bit the bullet of racist notions that Blacks were less intelligent than their white counterparts. However, this inequality has less to do with human endowment and more to do with opportunity. Black people experience the accidental disadvantage of living in a country that limits their possibilities; yet given the same opportunities of others, Black people are capable of soaring to the same existential heights as anyone else.

In *The Cornel West Reader*, West reinserts his version of prophetic pragmatism and summarizes its importance and usefulness for creative democracy. Following Emerson's lead, West calls prophetic pragmatism a new kind of cultural criticism:

> Furthermore, this new kind of cultural criticism—we can call it prophetic pragmatism—must confront candidly the tragic sense found in Hook and Trilling, the religious version of the Jamesian strenuous mood in Niebuhr and of tortuous grappling with the vocation of the intellectual in Mills. Prophetic pragmatism, with its roots in the American heritage and its hopes for the wretched of the earth, constitutes the best chance of promoting an Emersonian culture of creative democracy by means of critical intelligence and social action.[81]

With Emerson and prophetic pragmatism, West capably deploys radical democracy and individuality as weapons to combat the threats of non-being. Without a philosophical mechanism in place, these threats may persist as existential maladies depleting humans of ontological and metaphysical possibilities.

Given that *The American Evasion of Philosophy* is a genealogical analysis, West applies power, provocation, and personality to pragmatism, offering a reading of pragmatism that is more holistic. By comparing these Emersonian tropes to thinkers like Dewey, Du Bois, and Unger, West offers a reading of pragmatism that provides individuals with Promethean possibilities and creative democratic energies. The following lengthy quotation provided by one of America's greatest philosophers accents this point. In his essay "Pragmatism Resurgent: A Reading of *The American Evasion of Philosophy*" Hilary W. Putnam provides a final analysis:

> Emerson: West sympathizes with what he in one place (p. 216) describes as the "Emersonian themes of the centrality of the self's morally laden transformative vocation; the necessity of experimentation to achieve the self's aims of self-mastery and kinship

---

81. West, *Cornel West Reader*, 150.

with nature; and, the importance of self-creation and self-authorization." But he also tells us (p. 212) that Emerson's concerns with "power, provocation, and personality" need to be rechanneled "through Dewey's conception of creative democracy and Du Bois' social structural analysis of the limits of capitalist democracy." In short, West shares Emerson's sense that human individuals have Promethean possibilities. He sees Emerson as a figure who was "unable to engage honestly in sustained activities with agitators or reformers" (p. 22), but he is aware of the way in which transcendentalism was able (as we saw above), if only for a short time, to unleash moral energies to extraordinary effect. West, like Unger, thinks that leftist politics must value human aspirations to self-creation and self-realization, not denigrate or despise them as "petty bourgeois."[82]

West's liberal conception of the individual is one that implies authentic self-actualization and power to question and change to one's circumstances. This moment of self-actualization is a benefit of radical democracy, which resembles the creative democracy instigated by Dewey and is a notion that empowers all citizens. Dewey and West see individual moral agents as participants and agitators within social and political structures. Du Bois' critique of capitalism and Unger's promotion of leftist politics highlight the American problem of equality while accenting innate human capacity to change the world.

West's metaphysical agenda sees reality for what it is, something fluid and changeable. African Americans live in a democratic society but democracy has not always treated them kindly. Their experience supplies the index for dislocation, marginalization, and oppression. Thanks to West's metaphysics, African Americans, along with other vulnerable people, understand their value as individuals who are endowed with the wherewithal to invoke change. In other words, vulnerable people are endowed with Promethean energies to enhance the radical democratic project.

82. Putnam, "Pragmatism Resurgent," 19–37.

Discursive Dialogue and a Postmodern Ethic of Radical Freedom

Meeting Michel Foucault

Discourse and Discursive Dialogue

THIS CHAPTER BEGINS THE discursive dialogue between Cornel West and Michel Foucault, which sets the conditions for an ethic of radical freedom. As already suggested, the construction of ethical theory takes into consideration what ethicists believe about truth, knowledge, and reality. The ethics of radical freedom relies on notions of truth best articulated in the epistemology of Cornel West. Radical historicism and prophetic pragmatic notions of truth characterize West's epistemology. The tragic-comic, a genealogy of modern racism, radical democracy, and individuality, fall under one rubric, improvisational metaphysics. These foundational assets are critical to theory construction, yet some have areas of relative incompleteness.

For more holistic theorizing, I bring aspects of Michel Foucault's genealogy and archaeology into a discursive dialogue with these epistemological and metaphysical components. A method incidental to this theory construction considers praxis first, and though a paradoxical move, makes theory more palatable for conceptual consumption. With that, I begin with my initial encounter with Foucault's writings and their hypnotic effect on me, resulting in a dissertation and now this book. From there, I provide an overview of Foucault's work, and to stay consistent, I begin with his popular and practical appeal. Briefly, I provide some context to his initial philosophical development. This context is his early childhood experiences of trauma perpetrated by war. The conditions for the possibility of theoretical formation are angst, the threat of death, despair, and trauma. At the risk of overstating a case, I propose that these conditions contribute to the empathetic solidarity Foucault shares with subjects of discourse, and no wonder, beginning with his earliest writings, adjudication for those who are insane, patients, prisoners, and others under the control of power. I begin with my personal encounter with his work and its seductive impact on my conceptions of transcendence.

Meeting Foucault

Like the nagging thought that haunts the soul, serendipitous encounters abound, eventually calming an unquiet mind; such was my discovery of Foucault. "Going against the grain" depicts my professional and academic narrative, including my decision to leave the Church of Christ (which is extremely radical given its cultist proclivities—especially the African American Church of Christ),[1] pursuing a career in naval chaplaincy instead of full-time pastoral ministry, prematurely retiring from the Navy with seven years still left, and aspirations of pursuing a career in academia (which turned out to be harder than I thought). Yet my academic narrative is much more complicated and requires much more discussion, but in Foucault I found a kindred spirit who looks at discourse from a different perspective.

After years of graduate studies (ultimately comprising of four masters and two doctorates—actually a paradoxically unfortunate story), I encountered Foucault while matriculating at Claremont Graduate University. As the saying goes, one never knows what's around the corner, and after nine rejection letters to PhD programs, admission to Claremont, with a fellowship no doubt, arguably shows that deferred dreams do come true. And to make a long story short, my vocation as a scholar and ethicist begins with two consequential courses at Claremont: Introduction to Cultural Studies and Africana Studies. Both courses, apropos for a theology, ethics, and culture concentration, set the trajectory for years to come. Cultural studies, which had its own department and degree program, seemed then to be an academic commune of mostly Foucault groupies. His spirit seemingly penetrated this intellectual atmosphere. Completely a novice to Foucault or his work, I marveled at the intoxicating impact he had on students and

1. In all fairness I must say that many churches from this faith community do not maintain the myopic and parochial teachings I experienced in my formative years. In fact, my maturation and migration from this dogma began while at Abilene Christian University, a Church of Christ university.

faculty within this department. Ubiquitous references from presented papers, lectures, or just coffee shop conversations piqued my curiosity. However, given I was pursing a degree in religion, serious interest in Foucault waited for another two years.

The African Studies course, taught by art historian Phyllis Jackson, enlarged my understanding of Black feminism and enhanced my appreciation of postmodern theory and thought. Jackson, now my mentor and dear friend, was a huge fan of Foucault's *Discipline and Punish. A* proponent of postcolonial thought, Jackson resonated with Foucault's genealogical assessment of the normative gaze and his brilliant yet ironic presentation of penal punishment in Europe and the United States around the end of the eighteenth century. Jackson, an academic anarchist in her own right, brilliantly exposed the hypocrisy of the academy, which came at a professional cost. Yet her fearless confrontation of pervasive anti-Black racism in this particular academic environment fueled the Foucauldian flame blazing in my consciousness.

Fast forward two years, while working at the Naval Postgraduate School in Monterey, California, and due to distance and complications taking my final courses on campus, I needed an independent course. Thankfully, Patrick Horn, then philosophy of religion professor, agreed to an independent course on Michel Foucault. Alas, since taking the "cultural studies" course, I joined the gestalt of drunken Foucault groupies, an addiction from which I will never (nor do I desire to) recover. Existential freedom is at stake. Foucault heightened my attention to the myriad of ways power turns vulnerable people and communities into subjects of discourse, stripping them of their agency. As a white and French intellectual who has access to privilege, there are blind spots to be sure. However, his gift and ability to see the other side of discourse and his unusual acumen for exonerating marginal communities from historical pejorative perceptions make him a force for freedom. His early narrative, however, comes not with force but with fear. And it is to this I now turn.

The Conditions for the Possibilities of Phenomenology, Structuralism, Archaeology, and Genealogy

Like Cornel West, a public intellectual with celebrity status by the time of his death in June 1984, "Foucault was perhaps the single most famous intellectual in the world."[2] His writings appear in sixteen different languages, and his influence penetrates numerous disciplines like sociology, religion, philosophy, anthropology, and cultural studies, just to name a few.[3] Even nonacademics know of Foucault and his work. I am surprised by the countless people, upon learning of my interest in Foucault, who eagerly mention some familiarity with his work. His greatest appeal comes through his works on power and knowledge, but he also gets credit for being a parent of postmodern thought. Without question, the later Foucault possessed celebrity intellectual status only a few scholars experience in the span of a career. He died at fifty-seven with extraordinary accomplishments decades before, making him an intellectual with few peers.

Among the many things West and Foucault have in common, a few things are worth noting. First, most people know of their popular and more practical work with little, if any, awareness of their more theoretical texts. For example, the spellbound crowds West frequently seduces know little about the analytic philosophical rigor of his Princeton years. Similarly, as in my case, many first meet the author of *Discipline and Power* and the first three volumes of *The History of Sexuality* while being introduced to his analysis of power, knowledge, and truth. And for good reasons, because that's where Foucault is most relevant and compelling in this postmodern moment. Few know, or shall I say, hardly speak of, his two most dense and arguably theoretical books, *The Order of Things* and *The Archaeology of Knowledge*.

The second important commonality between West and Foucault is that both faced existential experiences early in life that shaped their philosophical outlook. West's early childhood knew of protest, anti-Black racism, inequality, and the destabilizing deaths of heroes like Martin Luther King Jr. and Malcolm X. West's preoccupation with the prophetic motif and redundant references to Malcolm X and Martin Luther King speak of unrequited redemption. As engaging as the discourse of power may be, perhaps for Foucault it is the culmination of a narrative riddled by discontinuity. Racism notwithstanding, Foucault's early narrative commenced with a childhood bereft of sustained political calm. Due to the crippling conditions of the Second World War, the old Roman town of Poitiers, where he spent his teenage years, knew of peril and death. With German occupation, war cries, and constant bombardment of bombs dropping, Foucault's

2. Miller, *Passion of Foucault*, 13.
3. Miller, *Passion of Foucault*, 13.

recollection was less than gleeful. This crucible of crises and chaos was like "spending one's entire childhood in the night, waiting for dawn."[4]

No wonder existentialism and phenomenology dominated the philosophical ethos of France during those years. Jean-Paul Sartre, Merleau-Ponty, Jean Hyppolite, Edmund Husserl, and Martin Heidegger were louder voices trumpeting notions of being, nothingness, terror, transcendence, and freedom. Indeed, existential phenomenologies were not mere trajectories of philosophical rumblings, but sources to make sense of crises and chaos. Knowledge of the construction and constitution of consciousness required attention. Foucault's orientation to philosophy commenced genuine questions about meaning and not mere abstract concepts or lofty notions in a distant land. Pedagogy had a purpose as the universe surrounded him with philosophers who vacillated between phenomenology and hermeneutics.

Later French philosophers found a new interest in language eclipsing the appeal of phenomenology and hermeneutics, thereby increasing the interest in structuralism and poststructuralism. This new interest, as James Miller observes, saw language, presumably, as a more pragmatic resource explaining structure. Where phenomenology focused on meaning as given by the human ego, language seemed to give a more concrete analysis of context. And though Foucault's earlier writings wrestled with phenomenological questions, his most noted earlier books had a structuralist bent.

The form of structuralism to which Foucault is most akin is diachronic or holistic structuralism, which does three things: first, it examines discourse; second, it examines elements within discourse; and third, it examines the laws and rules that govern discourse. In the book *Michel Foucault: Beyond Structuralism and Hermeneutics*, Hubert L. Dreyfus and Paul Rabinow note these similarities when they compare Foucault to holistic structuralism. They write in their introduction to this comprehensive text on Foucault's work:

> Foucault, as we shall see, explicitly distinguishes his method from
> atomistic structuralism, so we will be comparing and contrasting
> his archaeological method with the method of holistic structural-
> ism to which it is more closely akin.[5]

Dreyfus and Rabinow explain that, in holistic structuralism, elements within a particular system must be examined apart from the whole only for the

4. Friedrich, "France's Philosopher of Power."
5. Dreyfus and Rabinow, *Michel Foucault*, xx.

purpose of proving these elements as possible functions of the whole. Their case in point involves the work of structuralist Levi-Strauss who examines possible elements as they are detached from a system in order to see what elements are actually necessary to the overall system. Structuralists then individualize elements, and provide a table of permutations to see what elements are in fact actual to the larger system. In their own words they state:

> For holistic structuralists such as Levi-Strauss, all possible terms must be defined (identified) apart from any specific system; the specific system of terms then determines which possible terms actually count as elements, that is, the system provides the individuation of the elements.[6]

More simply put, holistic structuralism examines what individual elements make discourse possible.[7] Holistic structuralism also examines the rules that govern these elements within discourse, which allows discourse to speak for itself. When discourse speaks for itself, the philosopher does not force her own meaning and bias on discourse or on the participants in discourse. In this way, structuralism disagrees with the Husserlian notion of a meaning-giving transcendental subject. For Husserl and some phenomenologists, humankind is "totally object and totally subject," resulting in a transcendental ego that gives meaning to all objects within reality.[8]

In his text *Madness and Civilization: A History of Insanity in the Age of Reason*, Foucault explores the ambiguous conceptions of madness. Structuralism sought out semiotic relationships between discourse and language. In other words, language accounted for the inextricable depictions of discourse. He takes elements of madness and individuates them apart from entire discourses on madness. Concomitant with this overall depiction of madness is the language used within discourse. As the subtitle implies, depictions of insanity occurring during the so-called age of reason were tentative. Whatever individualized conceptions and depictions that are true of insanity, those elemental depictions are commensurate with the "age of reason." Foucault situates conceptions within different epochs. The

---

6. Dreyfus and Rabinow, *Michel Foucault*, xx.

7. In *The Order of Things*, Foucault examines Velázquez's *Las Meninas* as one of these tables of permutations. He refers to the painting as a table on which to examine particular elements within discourse. If the elements in the painting are true of a larger system, then elements in the painting are actual elements that underlie discourse. For more discussion, see Foucault, *Order of Things*, 3–16.

8. Dreyfus and Rabinow, *Michel Foucault*, xx.

discourse is madness or insanity, individualized conceptions depend on the particular epoch, which have validation insofar that there is commensurability with the so-called age of reason.

Three different periods occasioned three different perceptions of insanity, namely, the Middle Ages, the Renaissance, and the Classical Age. The Middle Ages viewed insane people as unstable and in much need of tranquility. As a consequence, with this age came "the ships of fools," and the embarkation of troubled and insane minds that wished to experience the calm precipitated by peaceful seas. The Renaissance viewed insane people as tamed, and on occasion, as diviners who provided rational insight. Good examples are the idiots and fools in Shakespearean plays. The Classical period viewed insanity as synonymous to criminality, which required mechanisms of supervision and control.

The Birth of the Clinic: An Archaeology of Medical Perception opens with an explanation regarding intent: "This book is about space, about language, and about death; it is about the act of seeing, the gaze."[9] Still structuralist in method, Foucault analyzed discourse in relation to political, cultural, social, and economic structures. And like *Madness and Civilization*, language fails to adequately account for discourse. Again, power of perception is tentative in that changing periods have different perceptions. Doctors presumably determine objectivity and scientific expertise regarding a "patient's body." Their gaze was absolute and rational. The body of the patient is the space of scientific discovery, yet aiding in medical advancement. Foucault gives an example of an eighteenth-century doctor named Pomme who treated a patient with hysteria by making her take baths every day:

> Towards the middle of the eighteenth century, Pomme treated and cured a hysteric by making her take "baths, ten or twelve hours a day, for ten whole months." At the end of this treatment for the desiccation of the nervous system and the heat that sustained it, Pomme saw membranous tissue like pieces of damp parchment . . . peel away with some slight discomfort, and these were passed daily with the urine; the right ureter also peeled away and came out whole in the same way.[10]

Thoughts about hysteria changed less than a hundred years later. Following Pomme's treatment, doctors observed an anatomical lesion of the

9. Foucault, *Birth of the Clinic*, ix.
10. Foucault, *Birth of the Clinic*, ix.

brain of the patient suffering from "chronic meningitis."[11] Pointing out difference of medical perceptions has less to do with the variety of ways doctors view patients and more about how history determines the conditions of these perceptions.[12]

The value of structuralism, in these examples, is its provisions for studying discourse through examination of elements within a particular discourse to understand disease in general. Problems come from the limitation of language to account for discourse, especially for a science of humankind. Foucault moves beyond structuralism due to language's limitation to account for a science of humankind, especially given the changing of perceptions during different periods.

Foucault changes his strategies from studying human beings and opts to examine the rules latent within discourse. This change of strategy begins the process of moving from structuralism/poststructuralism to archaeology. Herbert Dreyfus and Paul Rabinow appropriately subtitle their commentary on Foucault's work, *Beyond Structuralism and Hermeneutics*. The preposition "beyond" implies that Foucault retains some components of structuralism and hermeneutics without complete abandonment of structuralism and hermeneutics. Explaining how Foucault plans to proceed after some disappointment with previous methods, Dreyfus and Rabinow reason a way forward:

> We shall see as we follow Foucault's changing strategies for studying human beings that he has constantly sought to move beyond the alternatives we have just discussed—the only alternative left to those still trying to understand human beings within the problematic left by the breakdown of the humanistic framework. He has sought to avoid the structuralist analysis which eliminates notions of meaning altogether and substitutes a formal model of human behavior as rule-governed transformations of meaningless elements; to avoid the phenomenological project of tracing all meaning back to the meaning-giving activity of an autonomous, transcendental subject; and finally to avoid the attempt of commentary to read off the implicit meaning of social practices as well as the hermeneutic unearthing of a deeper meaning of which social actors are only dimly aware.[13]

11. Foucault, *Birth of the Clinic*, ix.

12. Foucault, *Birth of the Clinic*, xix.

13. Dreyfus and Rabinow, *Beyond Structuralism*, xxiii–xxiv.

As stated earlier, structuralism and poststructuralism have redeeming qualities and so does hermeneutics. The latter considers meaning and interpretation of institutions, social practices, and power. With the former, Foucault revisits subjects of discourse. With *Madness and Civilization*, the subjects were insane individuals, and with *The Birth of the Clinic*, patients were the subjects of discourse. Later, I offer "radical ontology" as an outcome of discursive dialogue, where subjects of discourse determine their sense of being by transcending established demeaning and pejorative perceptions.

Foucault employs archaeology as a method in his following books yet he still maintain aspects of poststructuralism in his next book, *The Order of Things*. The quotation below shows:

> which strata should be isolated from others? What types of series should be established? What criteria of periodization should be adopted for each of them? What system of relations (hierarchy, dominance, stratification, univocal determination, circular causality) may be established between them? What series of series may distinct series of events be determined? What series of series may be established? And in what large-scale chronological table may distinct series of events be determined?[14]

This quotation particularly reveals the influence of structuralism on Foucault's archaeology. This influence comes out in the way Foucault presents elements in a system or as the quotation above notes, "series," and then examines how these series fit into a "large-scale chronological table." But what's particularly next for Foucault is the middle ground between post-structuralism and archaeology with the publication of *The Order of Things*. As already noted, Foucault moves from an "objective" science of humankind to an analysis of the rules that govern discourse. Rabinow and Dreyfus suggest that the decision to move from a study of human beings to an analysis of discourse broadens Foucault's domain of investigation. They argue that this move was a natural extension,

> since Foucault had always been interested in how human beings understand themselves in our culture. Having first tried to understand how Western civilization attempted to consider and make sense of what was radically "other" about human beings, he now turned to the systems of self-understanding Western thought had

---

14. Foucault, *Archaeology of Knowledge*, 3–4.

generated through reflection on those aspects of human beings that were most accessible to it.[15]

Of critical note here is that Foucault keeps remnants of structuralism even once he moves on to a different strategy. In an earlier quotation from *The Archaeology of Knowledge*, Foucault mentions systems of relations that include hierarchy, dominance stratification, unifocal determination, and causality. He compares these systems to discourses on insanity and medical perceptions over different epochs. Hierarchy and dominance speaks of the overarching influence of experts, who through scientific acumen, determine what's objective about the insane and medical patients. The words hierarchy and dominance also reveal how some are made subjects of discourse. Foucault later addresses his concern about subjects of discourse in his genealogical writings, *Discipline and Punish* and *The History of Sexuality*. Enough said regarding the conditions for the possibility of Foucault's formative theoretical posture. I now bring him and West into a discursive dialogue.

Discursive Dialogue

I use the word *discursive* in a technical sense in that *discursive* refers to the intellectual resources used in theory formation. In *The Archaeology of Knowledge*, Foucault distinguishes between nondiscursive and discursive discourses, with the former referencing everyday interaction, whether through our conversations, practices, interactions, etc. At this level of discourse, we call it like we see it without having to refer to books, theories, or cultural and contextual analysis. In short, nondiscursive discourses and dialogues are surface discourses and dialogues. Discursive dialogue or discourse differs from nondiscursive dialogue or discourse as one investigates theories or the stuff that occasions theory. In Foucault's language, discursive discourse or dialogue is "archaeological." Literally, archaeologists are people who look underneath earth surfaces to examine artifacts that shed light on what we can actually see. When Foucault discusses archeology, he's being more metaphorical in that his interest, like literal archeologists, looks at the intellectual, cultural, political, and existential artifacts below everyday experiences and practices. Discursive dialogue gathers the artifacts that shed light on what we actually know or witness in everyday practice and experience.

15. Foucault, *Archaeology of Knowledge*, 16.

Hence, bringing Cornel West and Michel Foucault into discursive dialogue is deeper than a mere analysis of what they have in common or how they differ. West and Foucault in discursive dialogue is not an actual dialogue of sorts, where we pretend a conversation between the two. Discursive dialogue here means no such dialogue at all. If my practical reader imagines an eccentric African American wearing a three-piece suit, wild beard, and black scarf talking to a French, bald-headed, slim, and unassuming man having a conversation, then one misses what I mean by discursive. This point does not underestimate the need for such a dialogue and scholarship has to wait for that book. But this book on two consequential intellectuals and thinkers is means to a more theoretical end. Namely, this book constructs an ethics of radical freedom and in doing so, like the building of anything important, it uses components of both West and Foucault as foundations from which to construct this ethic of radical freedom. With this brief description, the next chapter begins the dialogue with reconstructing Cornel West's notion of truth and knowledge. This reconstruction relies on tenets of Michel Foucault's genealogy, most notably, his notions of truth, power, and knowledge.

CHAPTER 6

Discursive Dialogue on Cornel West's Epistemology

THIS CHAPTER CONTINUES WITH constructing a postmodern ethic of radical freedom by reconstructing Cornel West's overall version of truth with specific attention to radical historicism. As I noted in the previous chapter, radical historicism, though necessary for an ethic of radical freedom, has limitations which include a version, though thin, of objective truth; radical historicism also fails to incorporate power relations, making it hardly radical, if at all. With this weakness, I introduce the methodology of reconstruction, where I bring West's radical historicism into conversation with Michel Foucault's genealogy, resulting in what I call radical epistemology. That is, historicism, as a theoretical corrective and deconstructive tool to realism, representationalism, and "the given" situates truth contextually as well as historically.

One may ask why Foucault rather than another thinker who engages discourses on truth and knowledge? This reasonable question implies a potential arbitrary selection of two thinkers, but there is, in fact, intentionality because the ethic of radical freedom here is, theoretically, "postmodern." I say theoretical because one may think of a postmodern historical marker, which is to say, "after modernity." As a recap from the introduction to this book, both Cornel West and Michel Foucault are theorists who contest modern notions, and in this case, notions of truth, knowledge, and reality. West, as postmodern prophet, challenges the theoretical offspring to the modern Cartesian philosophy, and Foucault reconceptualizes pervasive modern conceptions like sexuality, power, penal systems, and insanity, to name a few. A postmodern ethic of radical freedom coalesces and mixes together postmodern ingredients, as it were, in establishing an ethic of radical freedom. With this we now turn to Foucault's genealogy, which similar to my discussion of West, begins with more practical discourses, eventually working our way back to theory. But I do with Foucault as I did with West, and that is, discuss my exposure to this extraordinary thinker whose influence cuts across many academic disciplines.

Toward a Postmodern Ethic of Radical Freedom brings two postmodern giants into discursive dialogue while, coincidentally, making two important correlations. First, both gained public appeal and popularity from the ubiquitous consumption of their more practical and accessible work. With Cornel West, people know and remember books like *Race Matters*, *Democracy Matters*, and *Brother West*, in addition to his celebrity status as a deep thinker and intellectual. Similarly, by the time of his death in 1984, Michel Foucault was by far one of the most celebrated public intellectuals who took the 1970s and eighties by storm, primarily due the polemic of power he discusses in *Discipline and Punish* and the first three volumes of *The History of Sexuality*. The second correlation is that their practical and more accessible work relies on theoretical formulations both made early on in their careers. West's prophetic voice, in part, echoes critiques articulated by a post-analytic philosopher. We see the same with the praise and applause of Foucault's polemic of power, which recycles the thoughts of a post-structuralist mind that is preoccupied with discourse. In conversations with nonphilosophers who have some familiarity with Foucault, these lay philosophers seemingly always refer to Foucault's more practical books: *Discipline and Punish* and volume 1 of *The History of Sexuality*. And though some may be aware of Foucault's more cerebral books like *The Order of Things* and *The Archaeology of Knowledge*, there is hardly, if any, awareness of the complicated and convoluted analysis these texts provide.

By the time we reach his more theoretical works, we see remnants of these theories and methods in Foucault's later writings and lectures. As I discussed above, one remnant is what Foucault calls nondiscursive discourse, which is the stuff that contributes to theoretical formation. By the title of the two practical books, it is an easy assumption that they are about punishment and sex, and to a lesser extent, they are. But more deeply, or discursively, they are about power, and to use technical language Foucault used in earlier more theoretical works, *Discipline and Punish* and the first three volumes of *The History of Sexuality* are books that entail an "archaeology of discipline," and an "archaeology of sexuality." In other words, the theoretical work of the early Foucault employed a method he called "archaeology." In fact, even earlier than the two theoretical books noted, are two other theoretical, though less cerebral, books: *Madness and Civilization* and *The Birth of the Clinic*. Here I gave the shorthand title, as I have with the aforementioned theoretical books, but showing the subtitles of these prove useful. For example, *An Archaeology of Medical Perception, An Archaeology of the Human Sciences*, and Foucault's critical text on the history of ideas, *An Archaeology of Knowledge*. In this last reference Foucault describes his agenda in the following way, and shows how the subtitles of these employ this methodology called "archaeology."

> It is these rules of formation, which were never formulated in their own right, but are to be found only in widely differing theories, concepts, and objects of study, that I have tried to reveal, by isolating, as their specific locus, a level that I have called, somewhat arbitrarily perhaps, archaeological.[1]

The publication of *Discipline and Punish* marks the transition from archeology to genealogy. The following clearly points to Foucault as a genealogist beginning with *Discipline and Punish*:

> the diverse studies of material grouped together in *Discipline and Punish* can only be closely analyzed when those studies are no longer seen as prompting a genealogical investigation of the human sciences, but as the consequence of such an investigation.[2]

Although Foucault eventually abandons archaeology as a means of understanding the human sciences, he does, however, rely on some of the techniques of analysis employed in the archaeological method. By the time Foucault publishes *The Use of Pleasure*, volume 2 of *The History of Sexuality*, he almost entirely distances himself from archaeology, but I think this is primarily due to his preoccupation with pure subjectivity. Pure subjectivity, from Foucault's analysis, requires understanding how people see themselves as "desiring subjects" and the need for constituting a domain of objectivity (as is the case with archaeology) is no longer necessary.

1. Foucault, *Archaeology of Knowledge*, 2.
2. Visker, *Michel Foucault*, 55.

A Postmodern Polemic of Power

Remember that an ethic of radical freedom brings Cornel West and Michel Foucault into discursive dialogue, which is to say, this ethic examines how components of one theory improves components of the other. Now that I have stated these preliminary requirements, I begin by discussing methodology and then pose questions for consideration. Therefore, this discursive dialogue between West and Foucault begins with this methodology and these (answered) questions in mind. I call this part of the discursive dialogue, a postmodern polemic of power, and to that I now turn.

To discuss Foucault's polemic of power, there are two critical questions for consideration. First, what does Foucault mean by power? Second, what is relationship between truth and power? Methodologically, we must see Nietzsche's influence on Foucault's later thought, more specifically, Nietzsche's imprint on Foucault's genealogy and conception of power. To be sure, an analysis of Foucault's notion of power is half-baked without this general understanding of the influence of Nietzsche on Foucault's method and its resultant "will to power." Nietzsche is one of the first, if not the first, philosophers to question acceptable truths of history. This kind of questioning opens ways by which Foucault situates his historical analysis so as to make the correlation between power and truth.

Anyone casually familiar with Nietzsche's seminal texts, *The Will to Power* and *On the Genealogy of Morals*, makes a minimal connection between Nietzsche and Foucault's usage of genealogy. For Nietzsche, this methodological technique explored alternative ways to investigate historical values in a particular context. A general exploration of his life and work, Nietzsche is often characterized as a nihilist, primarily because some (more so in conservative circles) see him abandoning morality altogether. But this is exactly the paradoxical point Nietzsche makes in *The Will to Power*, namely, that a moral disposition of absolute self-denial and abdication is itself nihilistic. Moreover, genealogy, for Nietzsche, reexamines history, pervasive moral positions, and discourses, and provides alternative ways of conceptualizing these conventions. For example, in *On the Genealogy of Morals*, Nietzsche reexamines moral notions of good and evil, showing how Judeo-Christian ethics changed these beliefs from their original connotations. Ronald Hayman notes, "Nietzsche overturns the unhistorical assumptions of 'English psychologists' that the idea of goodness was originated by those who benefited from altruistic action."[3] According to Nietzsche the notion of "good" represented nobility and the notion of "bad" represented slave or plebeian society. However, according to Nietzsche's historical analysis, Judeo-Christian slave morality inverts the notion of "good" and "bad" to "good" and "evil."[4] This inversion is fueled by the slave's resentment of being unable to take action, which results in imaginary revenge. In this way the weak "can feel superior to the strong, pitying them for what they will suffer in hell."[5]

Answering the first question, "what is power," Foucault discloses that power is ability to control belief systems, but even more interesting, are those who possess that control. Those who are under this control are, for Foucault, "subjects." The case in point in *Discipline and Punish* are prisoners, but in a very real sense, anyone under the unction of control are subjects. To answer the second question about the relationship between truth and power, Foucault asserts that truth comes through the relationship between knowledge and power. Proliferation of truth is necessarily knowledge and power. To this point James Miller asserts that Foucault, following Nietzsche, saw truth as a function of power and knowledge. Miller explains Foucault's conviction regarding power and knowledge by elucidating the themes that informed *Discipline and Punish*. On page 215 of the biography, Miller writes:

> Knowledge is an "invention" behind which lies something completely different from itself: a play of instincts, impulses, desires, fear, a will to appropriate. It is on the stage where these elements battle one another that knowledge is produced. It is produced not as a result of the harmony or happy equilibrium of these elements, but rather as the result of their antagonism, of their dubious and provisional compromise, of a fragile truce that they are always prepared to betray. Knowledge is not a permanent faculty, it is an event, or perhaps a series of events. It is always enslaved, dependent, and enthralled (not to itself but to whatever can enthrall an instinct, or the instincts that dominate it). And if it presents itself as knowledge of the truth, it is because it produces the truth, through the play of a primary and always reconstituted falsification, which establishes the distinction between the true and the false.[6]

3. Hayman, *Nietzsche*, 41.
4. Hayman, *Nietzsche*, 41.
5. Hayman, *Nietzsche*, 41.
6. Hayman, *Nietzsche*, 215.

This quotation unveils some provocative things about knowledge: knowledge is an invention; knowledge is not a permanent faculty; knowledge enslaves; and knowledge presents itself as truth. Foucault expands and elucidates these propositions in *Discipline and Punish* and the first two volumes of *The History of Sexuality*, with the overarching theme being correlation of notions of truth with power/knowledge relations. Like Nietzsche, Foucault has a great interest in production and proliferation of notions of truth. Unlike Nietzsche, Foucault gives attention to those victimized by these productions. Power produced knowledge, and truth is a by-product of this production. In an interview with Alessandro Fontana and Pasquale Pasquino, Foucault notes that all truth comes by way of power:

> The important thing here, I believe, is that truth isn't outside of power or itself lacking in power. . . . Truth is of this world; it is the product of multiple constraints. . . . Each society has its own regime of truth; its general politics of the truth. . . . There is a combat for the truth, or at least around the truth, as long as we understand by the truth, not those true things which are waiting to be discovered but rather the ensemble of rules according to which we distinguish the true from the false, and attach special effects of power to the truth.[7]

In *Discipline and Punish*, Foucault builds on Nietzsche's argument in *The Genealogy of Morals*, "and recapitulates its major themes with remarkable fidelity."[8] In his biography of Foucault, James Miller reveals that Foucault is doing in *Discipline and Punish* what Nietzsche does in *The Genealogy of Morals*; that is, he shows the correlations between power and truth. Yet Foucault's goal was the desubjectification of the will to power:

> Nietzsche's central concept—power—here, finally, claimed its rightful place as a central term in Foucault's own vocabulary: his political goal, as he now explained it, was "a 'desubjectification' of the will to power." To reach this goal required "revolutionary action"—a "simultaneous agitation of consciousness and institutions."[9]

---

7. Gordon, *Power/Knowledge*, 131. Originally printed as "Truth and Power," a translation of an interview with Alessandro Fontana and Pasquale Pasquino which appeared in Microfisca del Potere, reprinted in Gordon, *Power/Knowledge*.

8. Miller, *Passion of Michel Foucault*, 215.

9. Miller, *Passion of Michel Foucault*, 199. The quotations Miller uses are from Foucault's "Par dela le bien et le mal," 218–19.

Foucault picks up where Nietzsche leaves off, but with a more nuanced understanding of power. Whereas Nietzsche views truth and knowledge in light of the slave morality, Foucault presents truth as a result of a power/knowledge relation, which is an asset of the powerful, and at the chagrin of those being dominated. To carry out this "desubjectification," Foucault analyzes the penal system; however, not just the penal system, but Foucault also analyzes the power dynamics of educational and military systems as well. With the penal system as his major entry point to this analysis, Foucault "produced a genealogy of the modern morals through a political history of bodies."[10]

His book *The Passion of Foucault* contains a chapter, "An Art of Unbearable Sensations," where Miller connects the truth, knowledge, and power dots with the advent of the modern prison. Some may not see these connections, but if we trust Miller,

> for Foucault as for Nietzsche, "knowledge" was a by-product of corporeal powers, and intimately intertwined with an attempt to regulate these powers; the attempt to regulate power was, for both, tied to the prohibition of violent, cruel, and aggressive impulses, a prohibition enforced through punishment; both men hypothesized that such violent, cruel, and aggressive impulses, once blocked from external discharge, rather than vanishing, were merely driven inward—explaining, "no doubt," as Foucault glossed this quintessentially Nietzschean idea in *Discipline and Punish*, how "the man of modern humanism was born"—and how the soul became a "prison" of the "body."[11]

This part about the soul is interesting because the discourse on truth and power is a narrative of the body's treatment and how this treatment creates the soul. Foucault opens *Discipline and Punish* with a display of execution providing brutal details of the dismemberment and severing of body parts. This person being dismembered is an accused criminal sentenced to death by execution. Foucault gives step-by-step analysis of the execution in gruesome detail. The execution takes place for hours, stopping only if the criminal is willing to confess to a crime heretofore denied. There is some ease to the brutality of the execution if the criminal consents to "telling the truth" and admitting to the crime. This, however, does not stop the execution permanently. It merely halts it temporarily.

---

10. Miller, *Passion of Michel Foucault*, 241.

11. Miller, *Passion of Michel Foucault*, 214–15.

Afterward, Foucault gives an account of a seemingly gentler means of punishment. Prisoners ate decent meals, exercised daily, and enjoyed decent living conditions. Prisons were more tranquil and the threat of gruesome executions was no longer ubiquitous. Also, prisoners took classes, participated in competitive activities, and had means of employment. To be sure, this treatment was a kinder transition from the earlier means of execution.

If readers of Foucault's text think this to be a history of the penal system, they are mistaken. Neither should this text be read as a history of the treatment of criminal bodies. This text should be read as a genealogy on the production of truth and the way the "soul" is conditioned to acquiesce to forms of truth by constructing docile bodies. This history chronicles the transformative moments of the soul; it is, essentially, a history of the soul.[12] It is this history that also unveils the politicalization of truth by controlling the body of the criminal.

> The "soul" inhabits him and brings him to existence, which is itself a factor in the mastery that power exercises over the body. The soul is the effect and instrument of a political anatomy; the soul is the prison of the body.[13]

The "soul," for Foucault, is essentially a product of political power. The soul is controlled by first inflicting pain on the body and second by causing the body to be docile. Public displays of execution compel onlookers to respect and obey sovereign laws. Disobedience to these laws is an offense to sovereign leadership requiring retaliation from the king. The king's retaliation is based on a presumption of truth, the truth of the crime, and the details verifying that truth. At punishment, the criminal has the opportunity to verify the truth established by investigators of the crime in question. Mere accusation of committing crime implies at least gradations of truth, because the alleged criminal is always guilty and the mere presentation of evidence to his guilt is enough proof to execute or else he or she would not have been investigated in the first place. Therefore, the investigation process becomes a way of seeking for the truth owned by those possessing the power to make allegations. Foucault shows how power serves as the source for how knowledge and truth circulate; and in the case with public executions and

---

12. Foucault, *Discipline and Punish*, 30.
13. Foucault, *Discipline and Punish*, 30.

torture, power is exercised rather than possessed.[14] It is exercised because the body is the field of knowledge that showcases what Foucault calls a "micro-physics of power."[15] Micro-power conceives of the body

> not as a property, but as a strategy, that its effects of domination are attributed not to "appropriation," but to disposition, manoeuvres, tactics, techniques, constantly in tension in activity, rather than a privilege that one might posses; that one should take as its model a perpetual battle territory.[16]

The mere observation of the torture of the condemned makes observers passive in the acquisition of knowledge and how sovereign knowledge controls all knowledge. This is not entirely true, however, of the condemned or tortured person. They participate in the dissemination of knowledge and truth, although paradoxically. As Foucault puts it, the condemned person represents the inverted power of the king:

> At the opposite pole one might imagine placing the body of the condemned man; he, too, has his legal status; he gives rise to his own ceremonial and he calls forth a whole theoretical discourse, not in order to ground the "surplus power" possessed by the person of the sovereign, but in order to code the "lack of power" with which those subjected to punishment are marked. In the darkest region of the political field the condemned man represents the symmetrical, inverted figure of the King.[17]

The important thing to keep in mind regarding this micro-physics of power is that although the body of the condemned is the field displaying the interplay of knowledge and power relations, Foucault's genealogy shows the variety of ways the soul succumbs to these power/knowledge relations. And as is the case with *Discipline and Punish*, the field of this knowledge is no longer the tortured body but, following the nineteenth century, docile bodies are the field of knowledge. For this reason Foucault moves from presenting forms of punishment to presenting forms of discipline.

The second half of *Discipline and Punish* presents the conditioning of docile bodies. A docile body is one that "may be subjected, used,

---

14. Foucault, *Discipline and Punish*, 7.
15. Foucault, *Discipline and Punish*, 26.
16. Foucault, *Discipline and Punish*, 26.
17. Foucault, *Discipline and Punish*, 29.

transformed and improved."[18] Like the tortured body, docile bodies house the soul, but now the soul subscribes to notions of truth without possessing any power whatsoever. This poses an incredible paradox and that is, with seemingly more gentle ways of punishment, criminals have minimal agency over how they think and what they believe. At least the tortured individual determined what amount of established truth was verified. At any moment during torture, the individual could stop the torture by consenting to verify presumptions of truth about the crime in question. However, with docile bodies, the prisoner completely capitulates and acquiesces to what is established as truth.

Foucault demonstrates how docile bodies are controlled, and he does this by showing in detail how criminals are watched, educated, and conditioned. This means of control extends to the military and general education. In this regard, the penal system becomes the index for controlling the politicalization of truth. This politicalization takes place through power/knowledge relations. Dreyfus and Rabinow argue that unveiling this relation is where Foucault the genealogist really comes out:

> Foucault owes us a radically new interpretation of both power and knowledge: one that does not see power as a possession that one group holds and another lacks; one that does not see knowledge as objective or subjective, but as a central component in the historical transformation of various regimes of power and truth. This, of course, is exactly what genealogy attempts to provide.[19]

To make this clear and convincing, Foucault brings out three important means by which criminals were made docile, having minimal agency in how they thought and what they believed.

Criminals and citizens, respectively, are controlled by what Foucault calls hierarchical observation, normalizing gaze, and the examination. Hierarchical observation reminds prisoners of their invisibility to themselves and other prisoners, and it further reminds them that they are being watched by a sovereign eye, the guard on duty. Foucault describes this form of observation as a productive exercise of discipline. The exercise of discipline presupposes a mechanism that coerces by means of observation; an apparatus in which the techniques make it possible to see the induced

18. Foucault, *Discipline and Punish*, 136.
19. Dreyfus and Rabinow, *Michel Foucault*, 117.

effects of power and, conversely, in which the means of coercion make those on whom they are applied clearly visible.[20]

On page 200 of *Disciple and Punish*, Foucault introduces Bentham's Panopticon to further demonstrate means of surveillance and control. Bentham's Panopticon is a tower with windows around it located in the middle of a prison floor. With it, prisoners experience a sense of being seen although they cannot see who is seeing them.[21] For surveillance purposes, this Panopticon is no doubt one of the great modern inventions.

> Hierarchized, continuous and functional surveillance may not be one of the great technical "inventions" of the eighteenth century, but its insidious extension owed its importance to the mechanisms of power that it brought with it. By means of such surveillance, disciplinary power became an "integrated" system, linked from the inside to the economy and to the aims of the mechanism in which it was practiced.[22]

Normalizing judgment speaks to the discipline not only of prisoners but also of soldiers and students, and normalizing judgment also provides a standard by which to measure correct or incorrect thinking. However, individuals "are judged not by the intrinsic rightness or wrongness of their acts but by where their actions place them on a ranked scale that compares them to everyone else."[23] Implied in the notion of normalizing judgment is that there is a standard to which everyone aspires. Normal thinking is commensurate with notions espoused by dominant powers within discourse.

The examination is a combination of observing hierarchy and normalizing judgment. It is both a means of surveillance and a way to determine abilities and qualifications for promotions whether in school, in prison, or in society. In his description of examination, Foucault adds that examination

> establishes over individuals a visibility through which one differentiates them and judges them. That is why, in all the mechanisms of discipline, the examination is highly ritualized. In it are combined the ceremony of power and the form of the experiment, the deployment of force and the establishment of truth.[24]

20. Foucault, *Discipline and Punish*, 170–71.

21. Foucault, *Discipline and Punish*, 200.

22. Foucault, *Discipline and Punish*, 176.

23. Gutting, *Cambridge Companion*, 84.

24. Foucault, *Discipline and Punish*, 184.

Examinations require preparation and studying material given by a teacher (one who has knowledge) and a student (one who desires the reward that comes from receiving the knowledge owned by the teacher). In this way knowledge and truth are properties belonging to those who have the power to determine how, where, and by what means one acquires knowledge and truth.

With Foucault's assessment of truth, political forces are at work, and the reason we cannot remain with only radical historicism is that truth within context is also a result of this politicalization process. Each context is a subcontext of a larger context and the same power/knowledge relations at the macrocosmic level are at work at the microcosmic level.

The politicalization of truth is also revealed in Foucault's first volume of *The History of Sexuality*. This text shows not only the history of the truths of sexuality, but also how individuals discipline themselves in compliance with these truths. Foucault strikes a major chord as he opens *The History of Sexuality* with his ironic note, "We other Victorians." This note expresses the futility of any attempt to resist the discursive fixture of sexuality that Foucault calls "the repressive hypothesis." Indeed, the repressive hypothesis indicates acquiescence to a dominant and established understanding of the "truths of sexuality." We are informed that if repression has indeed been the fundamental link between power, knowledge, and sexuality since the Classical Age, it stands to reason that we will not be able to free ourselves from it except at considerable cost: nothing less than a transgression of laws, a lifting of prohibitions, an irruption of speech, a reinstating of pleasure within reality, and a whole new economy in the mechanisms of power will be required. For the least glimmer of truth is conditioned by politics.[25] The voices that dissent from the established notion of truth are the "other Victorians," and these Victorians stand at a distance from discourse, choosing for themselves their own thoughts about sex.

It was in the beginning of the nineteenth century that sex became domesticated and the truth of sex became a production of the Victorian bourgeois. Repression of sexual desires revealed acceptance of this production and a willingness to adhere to Victorian ethics. Resistance against this production was as political as was the act of establishing these truths. Dreyfus and Rabinow argue that it is no accident that the production of the truth of sex vis-à-vis repressive hypothesis was simultaneous with the

25. Foucault, *History of Sexuality*, 5.

rise of capitalism and the Protestant work ethic. Resisting the repressive hypothesis was a way of interrogating capitalism and the work ethic:

> It is certainly the case that, since the nineteenth century, speaking openly and defiantly about sexuality has come to be seen in and of itself as an attack on repression, as an inherently political act. After all, sexual liberation and the overthrow of capitalism are still considered to be on the same political agenda. By this argument, when we speak of sex we are denying established power.[26]

As is the case in *Discipline and Punish*, power is the mitigating factor in determining what kind of knowledge gets disseminated. Hence like the relations between criminals and power structures, there is also a power relations struggle taking place within sexual discourse. Whereas the recipients of the production of truth in *Discipline and Punish* are criminals and soldiers, the recipients of the production of truth within sexual discourse are the population adhering to protocol and acceptable behavior regarding sex. McHoul and Grace call this population "species," because it comprised a series of interventions and supervisory regulations concerned

> to govern aspects of life such as propagation, births, morality, contraceptive practices, the general level of health in the community, life expectancy, longevity, the natural conditions which can cause unexpected modifications of these processes (such as environmental factors).[27]

As noted above, beginning with the nineteenth century, sex became domesticated and the population species gave in to the rules of sex, vis-à-vis reproduction, privacy, heterosexuality, etc. Acquiescence to established truths regarding sexuality are best exemplified in what Foucault calls the "confessional." Foucault argues that beginning with the nineteenth century, sexual confessions came to be constituted in scientific terms. During the act of confessing one's sexual misdeeds, it is the one listening who possesses the power to forgive, console, and direct, and it was this act that precipitated the production of truth. That is, the production of truth came through this relationship of making the truth of sex (in this context) scientifically valid. The confessional can take the form of interrogations, interviews, conversations, consultations, or even autobiographical narratives. But where it is employed, it is a ritual that always unfolds within a power relationship.

26. Dreyfus and Rabinow, *Michel Foucault*, 129.

27. McHoul and Grace, *Foucault Primer*, 77–78.

Foucault points out that one confesses to a real or imaginary partner who represents not just the other party of a dialogue "but the authority who requires the confession, prescribes and appreciates it, and intervenes in order to judge, punish, forgive, console, and reconcile." The confessional is employed most readily within those institutions that bear on the knowledge of sexual practices: psychoanalysis, psychiatry, medicine, and pedagogy.[28]

Foucault's archaeological methodology is a useful way to examine discourse,[29] especially as it pertains to how people think about others as well as themselves. I see Foucault's genealogical methodology useful inasmuch as it examines power, in particular as power determines what people consider to be truth as well as the conditions that give rise to truth. The next chapter is an analysis of the archaeological and genealogical methods of Michel Foucault, which I use to reconstruct Cornel West's metaphysics and epistemology.

28. McHoul and Grace, *Foucault Primer*, 89.
29. Foucault, *Order of Things*.

CHAPTER 7

Foucault's Faith

Archaeology, Discourse, and Selfhood

THE SHORTHAND TITLE OF this chapter is "Foucault's Faith," and by this I reference Sartre's ideal of Being, and his appraisal of existential freedom to transcend static existence. What I mean by static existence is maintaining a posture that precludes flourishing. Contrary to Sartre's ideal of transcendence, static existence is what he calls bad faith. The ideal, then, is to transcend bad faith. Foucault embodies this ideal and refuses to be a hostage to norms, rules, and conventions that inhibit freedom and authentic existence. Sartre laments the "bad faith" of anyone who lacks authentic malleability. To this extent, Foucault does not disappoint, and his notions of archaeology, discourse, and selfhood, exempt him from Sartre's "bad faith." And to play with the Pauline New Testament passage, Foucault "walks by faith and not by sight."[1] In other words, he displays his faith by the content of his writings and changing positions through the course of his writings. Through archaeology and discourse, he questions theoretical and scientific norms that pervade historical consciousness for years. Foucault takes nothing for granted and compels his readers to do the same. Resisting grand narratives, offering an alternative history of ideas, or even freedom of selfhood, are formulas of faith.

Second, Foucault exemplifies the opposite of bad faith by virtue of his own example in that he will not be a prisoner of his own ideas. He changes methodology, position, and theory from one book to the next. Like

1. 2 Cor 5:7.

a fugitive running from justice, Foucault eludes his critics and sympathetic readers, changing positions and discarding ideas as if they were conceptual clutter. "Are you going to declare yet again that you have never been what you have been reproached with being?"[2] is the pretentious question Foucault poses for frustrated readers. His response is absolute confirmation he suffers from no "bad faith" at all: "Do not ask me who I am and do not ask me to remain the same."[3] As we see faith in motion, we turn now to the tenets of that faith and use them as resources for reconstruction.

Moving forward, I apply these theories and methodologies to formulate an ethic of radical freedom. I apply these theories and methods as reconstruction elements to expand on and improve West's metaphysics. More specifically, I first reconstruct West's "genealogy of modern racism" by applying Foucault's archaeology vis-á-vis discursive discourse. Although West's genealogy unveils the emergence of white supremacy in the modern world, his analysis is thin and incomplete. To be sure, exposing the "secretion of white supremacy" is an alternative narrative to racism's, and more specifically anti-Black racism's, lamentable legacy. Yet this genealogy does not account for the "possibilities of Black inferiority" and the myriad of ways Black people acquiesce and authorize their own subjectivity. Foucault's archaeology and, to a lesser extent, genealogy go a bit deeper and provide additional dynamics of discourse necessary for reconstruction. Given that Foucault exempts race from his writings altogether, his work alone is insufficient for an ethic of radical freedom.

I offer a more robust conception of individuality and radical democracy by the application to this concept of Foucault's "technology of the self." Individuality and radical democracy are two sides of the same coin, highlighting human powers to transcend "what is" in order to create "what ought to be." West's concepts of individuality and radical democracy—although a reasonable way to empower the least powerful, highlighting their intrinsic power to challenge institutions—are more ideal than realistic. Foucault's technology makes individuality and radical democracy more pragmatic by providing a mechanism that gives individuals agency over their self-creation. To begin this reconstruction, I define and delineate components of Foucault's archaeology, and to this analysis, I now turn.

2. Foucault, *Archaeology of Knowledge*, 17.
3. Foucault, *Archaeology of Knowledge*, 17.

Archaeology

We begin by answering the question, what does Foucault mean by archaeology? As noted earlier, there is some overlap between Foucault's post-structuralist work on insanity and medical perceptions. In his books *The Order of Things* and *The Archaeology of Knowledge*, Foucault explicitly employs archaeology as a method for discussing discourse, behavior, biases, convictions, and context. Metaphorically speaking, archaeology is the underground work that gives theory a day to shine. Theory shines, teaches, and informs, and provides a platform for practice. Archaeology provides the conditions for the possibility of theory. I now dive into archaeology to strengthen an ethic of radical freedom, particularly as it enlarges and improves individuality and radical democracy.

Archaeology entails *a grid of understanding*, which creates order and provides the inner operations of discourse. This grid of understanding configures practices, biases, values, and assumptions of a particular moment in history. In other words this grid gives order within discourse and provides

> the hidden network that determines the way they confront one another, and also that which has no existence except in the grid created by a glance, an examination, a language; and it is only in the blank spaces of this grid that order manifests itself in depth as though already there, waiting in silence for the moment of expression.[4]

Therefore, grids of understanding unearth forms of discourse. In *The Order of Things*, Foucault names this unearthing as "episteme." According to Chris Horrocks and Zoran Jevtic, an episteme is the "underground" network "which allows thought to organize itself."[5] Moreover, Horrocks and Zoran suggest that Foucault's notion of episteme is a "re-jigging of Thomas Kuhn's notion of paradigm."[6] The difference, I believe, is that epistemes are more specific than paradigms in that epistemes are conditions of possibility.[7]

Paradigms locate the foundations for modes of inquiry and essentially underscores transitions in thought. Epistemes are conditions that determine what rules control discourse, thereby providing the possibilities of experiences. For Foucault, each historical period or epoch possesses its

4. Foucault, *Order of Things*, xxi.

5. Horrocks and Jevtic, *Introducing Foucault*, 65.

6. Horrocks and Jevtic, *Introducing Foucault*, 65.

7. Foucault, *Order of Things*, xxii.

own episteme and, as it were, gives the face to that period. Theory emerges from the underground network of order, experience, concepts, biases, and presuppositions during a certain period. This is why Foucault calls this method archaeology:

> It is these rules of formation, which were never formulated in their own right, but are to be found only in widely differing theories, concepts, and objects of study, that I have tried to reveal, by isolating, as their specific locus, a level that I have called, somewhat arbitrarily perhaps, archaeological.[8]

In *The Order of Things*, Foucault used episteme as a principle to understand rules that govern ways of existing at different periods. In *The Archaeology of Knowledge*, he replaces episteme with discourse, and it is discourse (like episteme) that underscores historical unities, values, and goals.

McHoul and Grace explain that in *The Archaeology of Knowledge* two approaches characterized Foucault's approach, one formal and the other empirical. The formal approach examines discourse through text, giving particular attention to linguistic analysis and the social functions of language.[9] But this linguistic approach is only one side. The other side is mechanistic and "attempts to find general underlying rules of linguistic or communicative function 'behind,' as it were, 'imagined or invented text.'"[10] A best example of this mechanistic function is what John Searle termed "speech acts," which assumes that behind every performance of communicating lies a pragmatic competence governing discourse.

The empirical form of analysis is sociological and examines primarily the efficacy of commonsense knowledge, "which ultimately inform conversational rules and procedures."[11] This kind of knowledge is technical, or know-how. One good example of an empirical approach to discourse is "conversational analysis (CA), which bases analysis on an ethnomethodological approach to understanding discourse."[12] McHoul and Grace contend that Foucault thinks both the formal and empirical approaches have too narrow a focus. This narrow focus is on what Foucault calls the side of enunciation. Enunciations are "the techniques, the structures, the forms of

8. Foucault, *Order of Things*, xi.
9. McHoul and Grace, *Foucault Primer*, 28.
10. McHoul and Grace, *Foucault Primer*, 28.
11. McHoul and Grace, *Foucault Primer*, 29.
12. McHoul and Grace, *Foucault Primer*, 29.

know-how by which people are able to produce and recognize utterance."[13] This production and recognition examine only the surface of language and discourse and fail to effectively examine "what is being said" and "what can be thought."[14]

In *The Archaeology of Knowledge*, Foucault takes this problem head-on by introducing what he calls the "statement." It is the "statement" that captures the meaning of the discourse of a particular period, and functions as a network of rules that determines how we understand things. In a fairly complex and exhaustive introduction, he explains statements by first showing what a statement is not. A statement is not simply a proposition, sentence, or an utterance. These have different meanings depending on how and where they emerge. In different contexts, the same sentence may make different statements. A statement need not be a grammatical entity. Maps, which express statements, are not grammatical.

A final candidate is speech acts. Initially, Foucault argued that statements could not be speech acts, but later changed his mind on this position. Dreyfus and Rabinow argue that Foucault's position regarding speech acts has similarities with the position espoused by the philosopher John Searle. The main difference between the two thinkers is relative to the hearer of speech acts:

> Searle notes that speech acts have a literal meaning regardless of other levels of possible interpretation. Foucault too holds that statements are performances which can be taken at face value regardless of both the possible ambiguity of the sentences used in their formulation . . . and the casual factors involved in their utterance. . . . Searle and Foucault thus agree that the existence of literal meaning exempts us from having to look for deep meaning. To situate the statement the archaeologist needs only accept it at face value, and place it in its actual context of other surface statements. Searle, however, is interested in how the hearer understands a speech act. This requires more than situating it among other speech acts. To understand a speech act the hearer must hear it in a local context and against a shared background of practices which are not merely other statements. Foucault presupposes, but is not interested in, this everyday straightforward sort of understanding.[15]

13. McHoul and Grace, *Foucault Primer*, 34.

14. Foucault, *Archaeology of Knowledge*, 106–10.

15. Dreyfus and Rabinow, *Michel Foucault*, 48.

Thus, Foucault's interest in speech acts has little to do with everyday practices and the pragmatic background that serves as impetus for existing speech acts. Instead, Foucault is interested in speech acts that assert serious truth claims. In this regard, Foucault's interest lies with those who possess the authority to determine what operates as claims. When those who possess authority assert those truth claims, Foucault then says there are "serious speech acts." Unlike Searle, who has interest in the everyday speech acts that come out of the background of everyday experiences, Foucault focuses on speech acts that come from discursive formations. In my reading of *The Archaeology of Knowledge*, I believe that "speech acts" can only have meaning in light of these discursive formations. As Rabinow and Dreyfus suggest, I agree that

> Foucault develops in *The Archaeology of Knowledge* a method which allows him to avoid consideration of the "internal" conditions governing speech act understanding, and to focus purely on what was actually said or written and how it fits into the discursive formation—the relatively autonomous system of serious speech acts in which it was produced.[16]

This autonomous system of serious speech acts is part and parcel of the archaeological method. In order to determine which speech acts are serious, one has to understand the discursive formations that explicate meaning. The importance placed on discursive formations highlights one of the slight differences between archaeology and structuralism. The job of the structuralist is to find cross-cultural, ahistorical, abstract laws that define the space of possible permutations of meaningful elements.[17] The archaeologist seeks to "find the local, changing rules which at a given period in a particular discursive formation define what counts as an identical meaningful statement."[18]

---

16. Dreyfus and Rabinow, *Michel Foucault*, 49.

17. I pointed out earlier that Foucault uses holistic or diachronic structuralism. The other type of structuralism is atomistic, which examines elements within a system in isolation from the system at hand. Another form of structuralism is known as holistic, and it is this form with which Foucault has some affinity. In *The Order of Things*, Foucault examines Velázquez's *Las Meninas* as one of these tables of permutations. He refers to the painting as a table to examine particular elements within discourse. If the elements in the painting are true of a larger system, then elements in the painting are actual elements that underlie discourse. For more discussion, see Foucault, *Order of Things*, 3–16.

18. Dreyfus and Rabinow, *Michel Foucault*, 55.

For Foucault, the archaeologist has a twofold purpose. The first, one must understand as *discursive practices*. The second follows from the first, namely to discover the *nondiscursive* formations that give rise to discursive practices. This function gives serious attention to the serious speech acts that count as statements. One crucial objective of the archaeologist is to turn documents into monuments, which implies giving serious attention to what has "been said" and "what has been written." These discursive formations take on three modalities that determine the "unities of discourse." These unities of discourse are surface of emergence, authorities of delimitation, and grids of specification.

Surfaces of emergence are the social and cultural areas through which discourse appears. Good examples of surfaces of emergence are the family, work group, and religious community. Authorities of delimitation are the institutions with knowledge and authority, embodied in institutions such as the law and the medical professions. Grids of specification are systems by which different kinds of institutions may be related to each other. This modality constitutes a system of understanding by which one is able to see whether objects of discourse may be related to one another.

All three modalities constitute the unities of discourse and provide understanding of what takes place in discursive practices. Foucault uses discursive unities to see "by what right they can claim a field that specifies them in space and a continuity that individualizes them in time."[19] What equips one to do good archaeology is to bracket the statements of discourse (serious speech acts) by examining documents produced in a particular discourse and turning these documents into monuments. In other words, the archaeologist must examine speeches, books, oeuvres, and other materials, and from these gather "statements" that lend insight to the spirit of a context. The following and final quotation is from Foucault's words of admonition to the archaeologist:

> Before approaching, with any degree of certainty, a science, or novels, or political speeches, or the oeuvre of an author, or even a single book, the material with which one is dealing is, in this raw, neutral state, a population of events in the space of discourse in general. One is led therefore to the project of a pure description of discursive events as the horizon for the search for the unities that form within it. This description is easily distinguishable from an analysis of the language. Of course, a linguistic system can be

19. Foucault, *Archaeology of Knowledge*, 26.

established (unless it is constructed artificially) only by using a corpus of statements, or a collection of discursive facts; but we must, then, define, on the basis of this grouping, which has value as a sample, rules that may make it possible to construct other statements than these: even if it has long since disappeared, even if it is no longer spoken and can be reconstructed only on the basis of rare fragments, a language (langue) is still a system for possible statements, a finite body of rules that authorizes an infinite number of performances.[20]

From this quotation, we see that language is the conduit by which one grasps discourse. For Foucault, and other structuralists for that matter, one captures the efficacy of language through speeches, oeuvres, books, etc.—in short, through serious speech acts. Foucault moves from discussing the dynamics and the objects of discourse to discussing the interpretation of discourse and more notably the power structures that regulate how people think and behave.

This lengthy analysis of Foucault's archaeological method underscores the myriad of ways theory emerges, and how language, biases, and dominant and influential literature are part of a discursive domain. This domain differs from the level of ordinary practice and discourse, because no one sees discursive discourse with the naked eye, as it were. With everyday, or what Foucault calls nondiscursive, discourses, we engage in commonsense, run-of-the-mill, everyday activities with little reflection. Consider the racists' ideas of others, and that's without really seeing or knowing the discursive archaeological stuff precipitating these ideas. Generally, people are unaware of the infectiousness of serious speech acts promulgated through books, pictures, signs, commercials, advertisements, etc. In his genealogy of modern racism, Cornel West gets us off to a great start. But there is much more to consider, and it is to this consideration we now turn.

Reconstruction of Cornel West's Genealogy: The Problematization of the Objectified Other

West's genealogy offers an appropriate place to begin an understanding of some of the discursive factors involved in objectification as well as an understanding of the dynamics of racism in the modern world. He does this by employing a genealogical methodology. His goal is ultimately to expose

20. Foucault, *Archaeology of Knowledge*, 27.

the impetus of white supremacy in the modern world. West not only believes that the advent of modernity is concomitant with white supremacy, he also believes that white supremacy is what animates and energizes modernity. To understand the impetus of white supremacy, West asks the following metaphysical question: "What are the discursive conditions for the possibility of white supremacy?"[21] The conditions are essentially discursive practices that give rise to practical behavior and beliefs. West sees these discursive practices in the theories formulated out of the scientific revolution, the Cartesian transformation of philosophy, and the classical revival.

West notes that these discursive formations give rise to the emergence of modern racism, which comprises two phases. The first phase is the recovery of classical antiquity, which produced the "normative gaze." This normative gaze established aesthetic and cultural ideals resulting in established and pervasive conceptions of beauty. The discipline that gives scientific credence to these pervasive conceptions was natural science, which occasions the classification of human bodies.

> The principled aim of natural history is to observe, compare, measure, and order animals and human bodies (or classes of animals and human bodies) based on visible, especially physical characteristics. These characteristics permit one to discern identity and difference, equality and inequality, beauty and ugliness among animals and human bodies.[22]

Natural science is a theoretical foundation correlating whiteness with beauty while deviations from whiteness equate to a lesser beauty. And as this quotation implies, people are unable to dig deep into their psyches to understand why some people are believed to be more beautiful than others.

The second stage for the emergence of white supremacy is the rise of phrenology (the reading of skulls) and physiognomy (the reading of faces). These disciplines bolster the aesthetic ideal promulgated in the first stage by hitting home the notion that there is a science to determining superior beauty. Both phrenology and physiognomy suggest that cranial and facial measurements are foundational for determining beauty and attraction and that the thinner the face the closer it is to the ideal. Discussing the views of anatomist Petrus Camper, West helps to emphasize this point:

21. West, *Prophesy Deliverance*, 48.
22. West, *Prophesy Deliverance*, 55.

> Camper further held that a beautiful face, beautiful body, beautiful nature, beautiful character, and beautiful soul were inseparable. He tried to show what the "facial angle" of Europeans measured about 97 degrees and those of black people between 60 and 70 degrees, closer to the measurements of apes and dogs than to human beings.[23]

This quotation takes the aesthetic ideal even further than Greek classical notions of beauty noted above and correlates facial angle and size to character and soul. Giving these correlations, it is not surprising that white supremacy sets the stage for modern discourse and that pejorative depictions of Black bodies seem to be ubiquitous on the Western scene.

Strengths and Shortcomings of West's Genealogy

Overall, West's genealogy unveils the deep-seated discursive conditions of white supremacy and by doing so reveals the objectification of whiteness as a standard for beauty, intelligence, and morality. By implication, these deep-seated conditions for white supremacy point to the discursive conditions for Black inferiority.

To set the stage for a critical response to white supremacy on the Western front, West's usage of genealogy examines the logic endemic in the structure of modern discourse. In *Prophesy Deliverance*, West shows that with the advent of racism, the Western world adopted concepts of morality, intelligence, and beauty. These conceptions are indicative of a logic that is so deep within the Western psyche that for years their truth has been taken for granted. This logic, for West, manifests itself "in the way in which the controlling metaphors, notions, and categories of modern discourse produce and prohibit, develop and delimit, specific conceptions of truth and knowledge, beauty and character, so that certain ideals are rendered incomprehensible and unintelligible."[24]

As noted above, this genealogy implies the conditions for the possibility of Black inferiority, yet West sees "secretions of white supremacy" as critical to the emergence of modernity. West asks, "What are the discursive conditions for the possibility of the intelligibility and legitimacy of the idea of white supremacy in modern discourse?"[25] These discursive conditions,

23. West, *Prophesy Deliverance*, 59.

24. West, *Prophesy Deliverance*, 48.

25. West, *Prophesy Deliverance*, 48.

which are the impetus for the "secretion of white supremacy,"[26] come from such theories and superstructures formed in modernity. Hence, it is white supremacy and not Black inferiority that sets the stage for modernity. To be sure, Western philosophers like Immanuel Kant, David Hume, and Thomas Jefferson theorized about the inability of Black people to exercise sound reasoning and astute moral judgment. An unquestioning acceptance of such absurd theorizing underscores the construction and conditioning of thought. However, West sees the impetus of modernity to be white supremacy and not Black inferiority.

In his genealogy, West argues that there are structures of modern discourse that produce forms of rationality, scientificity, and objectivity as well as the constructs of cultural and aesthetic ideals. These structures lay dormant, as it were, beneath the domain of discourse making it easy to escape ordinary consciousness. West is careful to note that genealogy differs from the Marxist analysis of superstructure in that it resists making the connection between forms of economic production and power. In his own words West suggests the following:

> I am further suggesting that there is no direct correspondence between nondiscursive structures, such as a system of production (or, in Marxist terms, an economic base), and discursive structures, such as theoretical formations (or, in Marxist terms, an ideological superstructure). Rather, there are powers immanent in nondiscursive structures and discursive structures.[27]

The second valuable aspect of West's genealogy is that it highlights standards for beauty, intelligence, and morality. This aspect points to the emergence of the aesthetic ideal in the Western world, which consisted of "detailed observation, measurement, comparison, and ordering of the natural and human kingdom by autonomous subjects in the light of the aesthetic and cultural ideals of classical antiquity."[28] West discusses the discourse on the aesthetic ideal as the second stage in the emergence of white supremacy. This stage primarily occurred with the rise of phrenology and physiognomy. As noted earlier, these disciplines presumably prove that facial angle and size and pigmentation of skin determine beauty, intelligence, and morality.[29]

26. West, *Prophesy Deliverance*, 48.
27. West, *Prophesy Deliverance*, 48.
28. West, *Prophesy Deliverance*, 63.
29. West, *Prophesy Deliverance*, 57.

I see West's genealogy as a good start for understanding ways in which white supremacy dominates modern discourse and, by implication, argues for Black inferiority. Unfortunately, West's genealogy presents a thin argument for discursive formation of white supremacy, but, more importantly, it fails to show the objectification of Black people on the modern scene. The following is a reconstruction of West's genealogy using Foucault's archaeology.

West is right in constructing a genealogy of modern discourse by highlighting discursive factors such as the scientific revolution, the Cartesian transformation of philosophy, and the classical revival. West's genealogy studies modern discourse at what Foucault calls the level of scientific discourse. The mere notion of a genealogy (if Foucault and Nietzsche are right) is to study discourse from the perspective of power and knowledge relations. However, West wants to discuss discourse from the perspective of discursive formations and more importantly at the level of scientific consciousness. This is because West presents theories from white philosophers and dominant forms of scientific investigations. Recall that scientific consciousness takes into consideration the ideas and thoughts of philosophers and scientists who produce theories and concepts that determine the "normative gaze." Given that West assumes the position of genealogist, he can be of better service by studying modern discourse at the level of positive unconsciousness. Granted this level of investigation is what Foucault arbitrarily calls archaeology and, as discussed earlier, Foucault replaces archaeology with genealogy. Foucault's genealogy is helpful for an understanding of the relationship between power and knowledge, while archaeology elucidates discursive and nondiscursive treatments. And since West situates his genealogy within the metaphysical context of "understanding the conditions for the possibility of experience" (understanding discursive and nondiscursive treatments), he opens himself up for an archeological reconstruction of his genealogy.

As Foucault presents it, the archeological approach is at the level of positive unconsciousness that excavates the ground beneath theory and concept formation. This level of consciousness employs what Foucault calls episteme, that is, thought organizing itself. To invoke Foucauldian language, West examines the "episteme," that is, the grids of understanding, for white supremacy. However, instead of seeking to understand the conditions for the possibility of white supremacy, his genealogy will be better served if he examines the conditions for the possibility of the objectification of Black people. In employing an archaeological reconstruction of West's genealogy, let's reconsider Foucault's examination of the objectification of the so-called insane and medical patients. In the book *Madness and Civilization* Foucault analyzes these subjects, and brilliantly reveals how scientific discoveries (at the empirical level) about insanity and medical conditions reach objective status. And what results is the objectification of subjects of discourse.

The point I make here is that for West to consider discursive factors and in an attempt to highlight the problematization of modern discourse, the need is not a study of "the secretions of white supremacy." The need is a study of the conditions for the possibility of rendering Black people as objects. Herein lies the modern, and dare I say, postmodern problem. And at the archeological level of investigation, it is not white supremacy that is the impetus of modern discourse. Rather, it is the rendering of Black people as objects that is the impetus for modern discourse. Like the insane in *Madness of Civilization*, Black people are rendered as objects of discourse. Black people are rendered unintelligent, unattractive, and immoral. This rendering is the problematization of the objectified other and for the formulation of a postmodern ethic of radical freedom, Black people (and all people rendered as pejorative objects) must resist this objectification.

Radical Ontology: Reconstructing West's Radical Democracy and Individuality

This reconstruction involves primarily Foucault's text *The Use of Pleasure*, volume 2 of *The History of Sexuality*, which is a culmination of all the ways in which subjectivity is formed and of the powers involved in this formation. This text is most appropriate for reconstructing West, because it offers a conception of the individual who has absolute and complete agency in her own construction. In *Discipline and Punish* and the first volume of *The History of Sexuality*, Foucault discusses the systems that regulate power and consequently notions of truth. In *The Use of Pleasure*, Foucault discusses "the forms within which individuals are able, are obliged, to recognize themselves as subjects of this sexuality."[30] The power to reconstruct oneself or, if you will, one's ontology, is a nice addition to West's radical democracy and individuality.

In *Prophesy Deliverance*, West argues that Afro-American critical thought must consider the plight of African Americans and create effective ways to deal with social maladies such as racism, sexism, and oppression. His case in point is prophetic Christianity, showing how the tenets of this

30. Foucault, *History of Sexuality*, 2:4–5.

form of religion will prove helpful in bringing much needed liberation. This liberation will come about by incorporating individuality and radical democracy into his project. Individuality is the principle of self-realization, which enables people to fulfill their potentialities, to recognize their dignity as persons, and to realize their power to transform their realities. Radical democracy highlights, among other things, the dignity of persons, which accents the necessity of changing our circumstances. For West, individuality and radical democracy are two sides of the same coin. We need them working together if we are to bring about meaningful change in our context.

For radical democracy, the goal of individuals is to have a say in how their lives are governed. At the bottom level of the decision-making process, it is ideal to have a voice. As West notes in *The American Evasion of Philosophy*, individuals within a democratic society possess three important existential ingredients: power, provocation, and personality. Power is our ability and God-given endowment to transform our realities and to promote moral aims and personal fulfillment. Provocation is the means by which we are able to critique existing social and economic structures, highlighting both the bad side of market culture and the weaknesses of capitalism. Personality accents the dignity and worth of all human beings. West situates personality, particularly within the context of race, because history rendered Black people nonhuman. West's notion of personality reverses this historical understanding, highlighting the value and dignity of all people and especially Black people.

Given these characteristics of individuality and radical democracy, West thinks that we are fully capable of engaging and critiquing oppressive structures and ensuring a more flourishing life for vulnerable people, especially African Americans. In this way, these people can have agency. Similarly, individuality and radical democracy point to the power inherent within all people to question and challenge and to change what is to what ought to be.

The problem with this project is that it is idealistic. It is idealistic in that radical democracy assumes that people at the lowest level in the democratic process will actually be heard. History bears witness to the value of protest and the many ways in which protest changes laws and political practices. But, historically, protest typically takes place through groups (usually racial) coming together to fight for a common cause. The contemporary reality is that political resources are distributed in a variety of ways in African American communities. In other words, radical democracy assumes that all African Americans know the same political oppression and, moreover, have the same answers for political problems. Radical democracy conceptually is a nice place to situate a postmodern ethic of radical freedom. Indeed, individuality and radical democracy may allow vulnerable people to rally together and even protest oppressive realities. However, eventually protest and complaining gain minimal mileage in the face of the real problem: the conditioning that takes place at the discursive level.

I offer a reconstruction of West's conception of radical democracy and individuality in the following way. The process of changing a democratic society is to change a piece of the soul of democracy, one's self-formation. Foucault does well in showing us techniques of subjugation that have taken place, beginning with the objectification of insanity and ending with means of subjugation taking place in prisons, schools, and the military. The final technique Foucault offers and, as I appreciate it, the most telling, is the discursive techniques of subjugation and how we, as individuals, create ourselves in a way that continues to promote this subjugation. The protest is not against a democratic society, where the individual transforms what is into what ought to be. Rather, the protest is against oneself, removing from one's ontology all unhealthy notions that damage one's self-affirmation and worth.

Foucault presents this new technique in the form of desire and how individuals practice a hermeneutic of desire on themselves and on others. According to Foucault we train, condition, and discipline our minds in such a way that we learn how to desire. This is a telling technique indeed. Moreover, this technique exposes us to ourselves, and to a power intrinsic to our being. In the introduction of the text *The Use of Pleasure*, Foucault gives both disclaimers and methodology of this technology of the self:

> In any case, it seemed to me that one could not very well analyze the formation and development of the experience of sexuality from the eighteenth century onward, without doing a historical and critical study dealing with desire and the desiring subject. In other words, without undertaking a "genealogy." This does not mean that I proposed to write a history of the successive conceptions of desire, of concupiscence, or of libido, but rather to analyze the practices by which individuals were led to focus their attention on themselves, to decipher, recognize, and acknowledge themselves as subjects of desire, bringing into play between themselves and themselves a certain relationship that allows them to discover, in desire, the truth of their being, be it natural or fallen. In short, with

this genealogy the idea was investigate how individuals were led to practice, on themselves and on others, a hermeneutics of desire, a hermeneutics of which their sexual behavior was doubtless the occasion, but certainly not the exclusive domain. Thus, in order to understand how the modern individual could experience himself as a subject of a "sexuality," it was essential first to determine how, for centuries, Western man had been brought to recognize himself as a subject of desire.[31]

This technology of the self is a game of truth one plays on oneself in that one creates himself or herself as a complete subject. In the case of *Discipline and Punish*, the domain of truth and knowledge was the body of the criminal. With the technology of the self, the domain is the desiring subject and the discourse is no longer the history of sexuality per se. Instead, it is "the history of desiring man."[32] Individuals conform their appetites, sensibilities, and affections to a code of conduct and apply techniques to control their desires. This is what Foucault means by a hermeneutic of desire.[33] No need for guards, teachers, priests, or psychoanalysis; individuals are their own monitors and conduits of control. Foucault is keenly aware of how individuals turn themselves into subjects and *The Use of Pleasure* is a manifesto of freedom—releasing the individual from her own prison. In this manifesto, Foucault challenges readers to ask different questions. Elucidating Foucault's ethics, Bernauer and Mahon note:

> This view led him to ask new questions of himself and of the cultures he studied. How have individuals been invited or incited to apply techniques to themselves that enable them to recognize themselves as ethical subjects? What aspect of oneself or one's behavior is relevant for ethical attention and judgment (the ethical substance)? Under what rule of conduct do people subject themselves, and how do they establish their relationship with this rule (the mode of subjection)? In what type of activities do people engage in order to form themselves, to moderate their behavior, to decipher what they are, to eradicate their desires (the ascetics)? What type of being is one attempting to become by means of these ascetical practices (the telos)?[34]

31. Foucault, *History of Sexuality*, 2:1.

32. Foucault, *History of Sexuality*, 2:6.

33. Foucault, *History of Sexuality*, 2:5.

34. Bernauer and Mahon, "Ethics of Michel Foucault."

Unlike Foucault's earlier analysis and unlike his earlier quasi-structuralist position, the rules that govern discourse are no longer external to the subject. The subject determines her own conditions for the possibility of existence and in a real sense she possesses the capacity to jettison modes of subjugation. She is her own democratic system in that she decides how she will exist as well as deciding the constituents of a flourishing life.

Hence the answers to the important questions in the above quotation are implied in the questions themselves. In other words, the mere act of asking questions bespeaks a power intrinsic to "desiring subjects." These subjects participate in what Foucault calls the "art of existence." What he means by this phrase is that there are intentional and voluntary actions whereby subjects set rules of conduct for themselves, transform themselves, and "change themselves in their singular being, and to make their life into an oeuvre that carries certain aesthetic values and meets certain stylistic criteria."[35]

This technology of the self gives radical democracy and individuality existential value that individuals radically create themselves. This radical ontology evades social, cultural, and political constraints in that these constraints are external to our existence. If we are in fact constructed beings, then we must take control of our own construction. The lessons learned from Foucault's later works is that we have a moral responsibility to *not* abide by the rules of discourse, but our responsibility is to fashion our own existence:

> In these last works on the history of sexuality he probes a new axis of intellectual responsibility: in addition to the domains of power-knowledge relations, he excavates a specific axis of the relationship to oneself, the ways we fashion our subjectivity. . . . This axis of subjectivity refers to the set of practices we perform on ourselves, and for Foucault ethics is essentially a mode of self-formation, the way we fashion our freedom.[36]

Like the criminal in *Discipline and Punish*, we possess the power to determine truth and meaning for ourselves. As noted in the discussion of that text, the condemned person owns some power and agency. And as noted regarding Foucault's notion of the "analytic of power," power is not merely from the top down but from the bottom up.

---

35. Foucault, *History of Sexuality*, 2:10–11.

36. Bernauer and Mahon, "Ethics of Michel Foucault," 143.

CHAPTER 8

A Postmodern Ethic of Radical Freedom

Radical Ontology, Radical and Womanist Epistemology

THIS CHAPTER IS THE culmination of all the discursive work heretofore discussed, bringing us to "radical freedom." Two trajectories make up radical freedom, and they are *radical ontology* and *radical epistemology*. Using personal experiences and other examples to show the importance of these components, they are the reconstructive outcomes of West's radical historicism, genealogy, radical democracy, and individuality. I use Foucault's conception of the historical subject to build on West's genealogy. This conception not only highlights ways in which vulnerable people are rendered inferior, but it empowers so-called objects of discourse to have more agency in how they view themselves. Foucault's conception of truth provides a more robust understanding of radical historicism in that truth claims espoused by a local community as well as the individual within community are always suspect, given that these claims may result from power/knowledge relations. Foucault's "technology of the self" enhances West's radical democracy and individuality by affording vulnerable individuals with the tools to recreate themselves, such that they are able to flourish in the face of "external social and political constraints." I begin with radical ontology, and its usefulness to combat pejorative understandings not only of Black people, but also of anyone who is negatively rendered as objects of discourse.

I started this book with my personal religious narrative growing up in Chattanooga, Tennessee, and showed undercurrents of theory formation. In this final chapter I want to begin like I started and give another personal experience that I think demonstrate the efficacy of an ethic of radical freedom. Unlike the positive ones that set the trajectory of theory formation through practical observations, this narrative, though necessary, has lamentable circumstances. Sadly enough, it is a narrative that symbolizes many students, professionals, professors, etc., who endure anti-Black racism daily.

Putting Theory into Practice: What's Radical about Radical Freedom?

The things we say out loud to people become the conditions in constructing consciousness, and those on the receiving end will have to work hard to transcend a resulting negative self-consciousness. Negative notions we have about people and about ourselves lack empirical validation. Rather, these notions have life through social, existential, and cultural constructions. Without immediate provocation, we deem people lazy, intellectually weak, immoral, highly sexed, criminal, loud, unattractive, dangerous, and so on. Objectifications like these rarely come from real observations and experience from those who believe them. To add insult to this injury, even those on the unfortunate side of these objectifications accept these negative notions as true. Xenophobic ideals appear to have an elongated existence. For those rendered objects will have to work around political, cultural, and social constraints and figure out how to leap beyond the subjective absurdity imposed by these constraints. This transcendence is what I call radical ontology. Radical ontology is a reconfiguration of one's sense of "being" in these destructive and demoralizing spaces.

In a personal reflection, I know that such transcendence is possible. I experienced objective rendering, where I had to wage internal war with my value and self-worth. And to be honest the war still goes on not just with me, but with others seeking acceptance and a chance to prove and demonstrate their worth. I turn now to two examples. The first is an experience of a failing grade I received on my comprehensive master's exam in philosophy, which from my understanding was the first for that department. The second was from an analytic philosophy class I took at a university in hopes of entering its PhD program. I begin with the experience of failing a comprehensive exam for my master's degree in philosophy.

Three emotionally draining and existentially exhausting years end with the master's exam, which determines competence for a master's level philosophy degree. The day of the comprehensive exam, the professor assigned to both proctor and grade part of the exam engages in what could be construed as casual conversation right before he gives me the exam. While waiting for the exam room to become available, he asks, "What will you do if you fail the exam?" Being aware that in the next week I begin my career as a navy chaplain, he feels this is a fair question, giving my immanent change in location and occupation. However, the question, which is certainly untimely (right before I am to take the exam), informs me that he has entertained the possibility that I may fail the exam. And given that no one in the history of the department has ever failed the master's exam, such a question was hardly warranted. So it was not too surprising to me when I, the only African American student in the program at that time, and the second one in the history of the program, failed the exam. Word of my failure came while in officer training in Newport, Rhode Island, and though I want to say I was surprised, I had enough sense to know if my proctor had already entertained failure, the other graders would follow. Later I will discuss how this failure is also my fault, though not due to preparation.

The second experience takes place four years later when I took an "introduction to analytic philosophy" class at a fairly reputable university, which had a very respectable philosophy program. The first written assignment was a comparable analysis of Bertrand Russell's and A. J. Ayer's notion of "definite descriptions." To say that the assignment was difficult is an understatement, and the day the professor returned the papers, she noted that with one exception, everyone failed the written assignment. Although mostly every student in the class failed this written exam, I was the only student she required to come to see her to discuss my work. During our meeting, she acknowledged her concerns about my ability to do graduate philosophy and that perhaps analytic philosophy is not a subject easily grasped by African Americans. To further prove her point that race and ethnicity were sufficient conditions for doing (or not doing) analytic philosophy, she noted that the Asian (I cannot remember the specific country) student in the class was the only person who passed the written assignment, also lauding the superior intelligence of Asians who attend American universities. Conversely, she implied that African Americans lacked the ability bequeathed to Asians, with the clear point, "you are in the wrong discipline." To add insult to injury, for the next several weeks I questioned whether I possessed the aptitude necessary for doing academic analytic philosophy. The philosophy master's degree I had earned just three years prior—I passed the exam on the second try—was not enough to break either of us away from the pejorative objectification of Black intelligence. Both of us accepted *a priori* notions concerning Black intelligence, namely, African Americans were intellectually inferior to other races. Although the two-page paper on Russell and Ayer was hardly enough to verify my inability to do philosophy, she assumed that Blackness was the mitigating factor for a poorly written paper—although every paper in the class, regardless of the students' race, failed to meet her expectations.

My first moment of radical ontology came after these two unfortunate events, and I realized that in order to excel academically, I needed to resist pejorative forms of objectification and instead reconstruct my sense of self. This reconstruction entailed a conception of Black intelligence that eschews discursive notions of Black inferiority. I also needed to adopt the nondiscursive practice of self-affirmation. In other words, I recreated myself by determining the "conditions for the possibility of experience." My first exercise was to speak to myself out loud and verbalize a "no" to the negative things that were either said or implied. Second, I literally spoke to myself in positive ways that affirmed my intelligence. During my hour drive to the campus, I said to myself over and over again "I am brilliant." Whether I was/am brilliant is secondary to the nondiscursive practice of affirming my intelligence. And although it may be coincidental, subsequent to those horrible experiences at these two universities, nine months later I applied and received admission to Yale University. The two years at Yale enjoyed more academic success than any graduate experience prior. I have received a master's degree from Yale University (with philosophy classes earning the grade of A) and later received admission to Claremont, perhaps partly due to the recommendations from the great feminist and womanist theologian Letty Russell and then Yale University Chaplain Frederick J. Streets. What I learned is that radical freedom means being an agent in how I see myself and perhaps how others see me.

In addition to these successes was one that seems almost like poetic justice but in a very real sense, a clear indication of the power of transcendence and radical ontology. Recall that I failed the master's exam a decade earlier at a school that pales in comparison to the reputation of Claremont—at least according to university rankings. For Claremont, prior to admission to candidacy, students in the school of religion must pass a qualifying exam that consists of four major areas or thinkers. Each exam is four hours, and the exams are taken over a period of a month. Given my schedule, I took each exam a week at a time. Upon finishing the final exam, the student then schedules an oral exam and after passing the oral exam, the student then advances to candidacy. I asked a professor about the rationale for the oral exam, and he replied that given the intensity and time crunch of written exams, it's nearly impossible to sufficiently answer the four written exam questions. Consequently, the oral exam gives students a chance to demonstrate breadth of knowledge and to compensate for missing pieces on the written exam. To make a long story short, I went to sit for my oral exam. This exam begins with the four professors who graded the written exam collaborating on how to proceed. They speak together about areas that require further explanation and then agree on the questions for the oral exam. Then they bring the student into the room for questioning, and after an hour or so send the student out as they deliberate. When I come into the room to sit for the oral exam, to my surprise my advisor informs me that there is no need to take the oral exam at all. Seeing the perplexity in my facial expressions, she says, "That's right, you answered every question to our satisfaction, and you passed the qualifying exam. So there is no need for an oral exam." I mention this experience not as a moment for self-aggrandizement, but to show the power of radical ontology. Recreating oneself ushers in a sense of being that can and will transcend any and all constraints.

Therefore, *Toward a Postmodern Ethic of Radical Freedom* offers to readers, especially those who share experiences similar to mine, a pilgrimage to an existential promised land where vulnerable people enjoy flourishing despite the accidents of birth and having to occupy, through no fault of their own, spaces beyond their control. Indeed, we cannot control pervasive racism as well as anti-Black sentiments, sexism, classism, and ableism. Like Reinhold Niebuhr, I believe that it is too ambitious, and perhaps even naïve, to believe you can expunge prejudices from the hearts of individuals and collectives who enjoy social and political advantages. Even years after Niebuhr's *Moral Man and Immoral Society*, privileged groups tiptoe through social justice terrain. History testifies that groups will hardly trade power for egalitarian equality. Liberation and freedom move at turtle speed despite liberal optimism to the contrary. And with overt racism, religious bigotry, homophobia, anti-Islamic sentiments coming from the most senior political leaders, positive change is nowhere in sight. Yes, after George Floyd's murder, massive international demonstrations seemed to imply that we were witnessing in real time the death of anti-Black racism.

How interesting is it, however, that adjudication of institutional and systemic anti-Black racism comes because people publicly acknowledge the obvious. Of course, literally, Black lives, or even all lives, matter. Intuitively, you know that killing another human being in broad daylight is egregious and unacceptable. To be sure, George Floyd and countless Black and Brown men and women did not deserve to die when they posed no threats to their murderous perpetrators. But it doesn't take rocket science to know that their lives matter. My question is, does solidarity subside once adrenalin calms a bit? Once the nostalgia that public protest produces wanes, will there be residual resistance to anti-Blackness when returning to private and professional spaces? Will Black lives matter upon retreat to spaces where real life matters? When there is no crowd, will advocacy of Black lives matter in your work spaces like higher education and corporate America where covert anti-Black racism lives everyday? Notwithstanding personal testimony, many of my Black friends in academia, for example, lament how doors shut to tenure, hiring, and promotion by people who deny compliance to the assassination of Black lives. Authentic freedom and liberation occur upon removal of barriers that preclude well-being and flourishing. Suffice to say that institutional and systemic anti-Black racism will not be on hospice anytime soon. Black people need freedom without a doubt, but they do not have a monopoly on misfortune. Many more communities fight the fight for justice, seeking liberation from constraints that hinder freedom and flourishing. Concomitant with the slow death of anti-Black racism are a myriad of social misfortunes that preclude well-being. Literally, the moral of this bantering and righteous indignation is clearly the revelation that external freedom may come slowly, if ever. Waiting for xenophobia to reach its end parallels the perennial impatience of waiting for Godot.

While we wait, existential freedom will suffice in the meantime. Existential freedom requires the soul to access its power to transcend constraints and conditions that block opportunities (or not) in a democratic society. *Toward a Postmodern Ethic of Radical Freedom* is hopefully a resource and a guide to acquiring flourishing and fulfillment.

Anti-Black racism is alive and has momentum commensurate with any time in history, and a key reason is the negative depictions of "Blackness." Postmodernity objectifies Black people, thereby rendering them, at times, intellectually, morally, and aesthetically inferior. This objectification extends to a myriad of professional contexts, including academia. J. Cole's rap song "My Neighbors Think I'm Selling Dope" echoes the bewailing cry of Black men and women whose professional and intellectual acumen seems, at times, to the normative gaze, to represent low-brow musings. J. Cole's song brilliantly laments how this normative gaze reduces the Black genius to nothing but dope selling. Which is to say that Black intellectual discourse (perhaps across many disciplines) is at best merely revisionist input and at worst, marginally adequate to the intellectual industry. *Toward a Postmodern Ethic of Radical Freedom* provides a polemic against such assumptions. In so doing, I agree with J. Cole's artistic allegation and argue that Black intellectual discourses, in their myriad of forms, are too often reduced to "selling dope." An ethic of radical freedom is a discursive analysis insofar as it looks at the deeper levels of (intellectual) discourse and asks the metaphysical question, "What are the conditions for the possibility of presuming Black intellectual inferiority?" This is where West and Foucault help. In his earlier archaeological work, Foucault examined the myriad of ways marginalized people were rendered as historical and helpless objects. This rendering results from normative gazing, as it were, and turns historical objects into historical subjects.

This chapter is the constructive work, where I present a postmodern ethic of radical freedom as well as provide implications for this ethic. This chapter lays out the two components of my ethical project. The first part briefly explains what I mean by "postmodern" and "radical freedom." Regarding the notion of postmodern, I make a distinction between postmodern as a historical marker vis-à-vis after modernity and postmodern as theoretical discourse. I prefer the latter to the former. I argue that radical freedom entails two critical trajectories, namely, radical epistemology and radical ontology.

The second part is an elucidation and highlighting of the implications of these trajectories. In the case of radical ontology, I argue that African Americans must define their own identity and resist pejorative perceptions and conceptions that render them inferior. Regarding radical ontology, I argue that African Americans must have complete autonomy—in other words absolute control—over the way they live their lives. Employing West's metaphysics of individuality and radical democracy along with Foucault's technology of the self, radical ontology denotes a sense of being in the world such that African Americans exercise the power they have to change their social and existential circumstances. Regarding radical epistemology, I argue that African Americans embrace only those truth claims that affirm selfhood and value. African Americans must reject any truth claims that negate selfhood and this rejection happens regardless of the context (vis-à-vis church, community, and family).

Postmodern

I choose to view myself as a "postmodern" theorist and believe that my convictions regarding objective truth, metanarratives, and subjectivity are commensurate with thinkers who are considered postmodern. More specifically, my view of the notion of postmodernity draws upon the works of two postmodern geniuses, Cornel West and Michel Foucault. Although Cornel West and Michel Foucault resist this depiction, both thinkers employ postmodern themes of subjective truth claims, negation of metanarratives, and radical ontology in their works. Both philosophers employ genealogy as an interpretive methodology; both philosophers question presumptions of objective truth; and both philosophers resist metanarratives. I call this a postmodern ethic for these three reasons. In my Foucauldian reconstruction of West, I see these themes as critical resources for philosophical ethics.

My conception of "postmodern" falls within the tradition of what is known as Black postmodernism, because I deny Black essentialism and believe that the notion of Blackness is neither a necessary nor a sufficient condition for identity. Blackness is a social construct and is the Blackness that whiteness created. That being the case, a postmodern ethic of radical freedom removes pejorative lenses and argues that African Americans determine their identity while, at the same time, using Blackness as regulative. To use Blackness as regulative means to take this assigned racial depiction and recreate individual identity in a more positive way.

In her essay "Postmodern Blackness," bell hooks argues that Black scholars must resist the temptation of thinking and writing of Blackness in essentialist terms. Postmodern Blackness highlights difference and otherness, showing that racist conceptions are absurd when considering the multiple identities African Americans possess. She states:

> Employing a critique of essentialism allows African-Americans to acknowledge the way in which class mobility has altered collective black experience so that racism does not necessarily have the same impact on our lives. Such a critique allows us to affirm multiple black identities, varied black experience. It also challenges colonial imperialist paradigms of black identity which represent blackness one-dimensionally in ways that reinforce and sustain

white supremacy. This discourse created the idea of the "primitive" and promoted the notion of an "authentic" experience, seeing as "natural" those expressions of black life which conformed to a pre-existing pattern or stereotype. Abandoning essentialist notions would be a serious challenge to racism. Contemporary African-American resistance struggle must be rooted in a process of decolonization that continually opposes reinscribing notions of "authentic" black identity. This critique should not be made synonymous with the dismissal of the struggle of oppressed and exploited peoples to make ourselves subjects. Nor should it deny that in certain circumstances that experience affords us a privileged critical location from which to speak. This is not a reinscription of modernist master narratives of authority which privilege some voices by denying voice to others.[1]

Hooks dismisses essentialism, because essentialism sees Black identity as one-dimensional and holds all Black people hostage to the certain proclivities and tendencies of a few. Notions that seem positive, like "all African Americans have rhythm" are just as problematic as the notion that "African Americans are more practical thinkers than abstract thinkers." Even in lauding the gifts of African Americans, Black postmodern thinkers must not fall prey to the mistake made by modernist thinkers; namely, employing master narratives that lump all African Americans into one homogeneous blob.

In conclusion, this constructive proposal is postmodern in that it highlights the variety of ways in which we think and conceive of ourselves. Postmodernity is itself a radical trajectory in that it seeks to transcend normative notions of selfhood, freedom, and individual contribution to community and context. To this extent, the constructive model employed here is undergirded by the postmodern concerns heretofore discussed.

Radical Ontology and the Creation of the Self

The final component of radical freedom is radical ontology where (African American) individuals are the agents of their own creation and consequently exercise their God-given power to instigate change to their realities in the face of social, cultural, and political constraints. To be sure, social, cultural, and political constraints may be in tension with individual flourishing and fulfillment, but such tension will result in a technology of the

---

1. hooks, "Postmodern Blackness."

self that empowers individuals to be the masters of their own fates. That being stated, this section will involve three trajectories. The first trajectory is the tension between internal constraints and external constraints, providing a strategy whereby the former attempts to overcome the latter. The second trajectory is an outcome of the first trajectory. Overcoming internal constraints gives individuals the wherewithal to interrogate external constraints. This endeavor is the catalyst for social activism, and social activism serves as a possibility for change. However, I conclude that social activism is a necessary condition for change and not a sufficient condition for change. The third trajectory builds on the second, and that is what is of ultimate importance for radical ontology—"recreation of oneself," which involves Foucault's brilliant notion of "the technology of the self." I now discuss the first trajectory, beginning with Cornel West's metaphysics of radical democracy and individuality.

Radical ontology claims that radical democracy and individuality are critical in that both seek ways to remedy social and political pain. There are external constraints imposed upon those who are vulnerable. These constraints proliferate second-class citizenship, sexism, racism, heterosexism, and other social maladies. It may be hard to actually overcome all constraints, but the first step is to remove the internal constraints that also impede progress. This is where Cornel West's metaphysic of radical democracy and individuality is helpful.

Radical democracy and individuality serve as the benchmark for authentic living by offering ways to change oppressive realities. In this way, the metaphysic of radical democracy and individuality serves as a means of existential and social protest. Radical democracy denotes the political power given to all citizens, who, by virtue of being human, have a right to speak to their plight in a democratic society. Radical democracy speaks to the importance of vulnerable people of raising their most critical democratic concerns and of interrogating political powers that may overlook these concerns. Individuality denotes the existential freedom that all people have to transcend their realities and not give in to despair. This existential freedom precipitates social freedom inasmuch as social freedom cannot happen until vulnerable people realize the power bequeathed to them as human beings and agents of their own destiny.

As West points out in *Prophesy Deliverance*, radical democracy and individuality are moral norms implying that we must not only know the constraints that preclude democratic possibilities, but that we are obliged to make worthy attempts to change our realities. Radical democracy and individuality are moral edicts showing that we can transform what is to what ought to be and requiring that we act. Although this endeavor may not always result in actual change, West still believes that we must strive to transform our existential realities. Given that change is not inevitable, West claims he is not always optimistic.

Optimism is naïve given that things may not always be favorable. Yet hope at least allows us to exercise our God-given powers to make attempts at changing things. However, it is one thing for an individual to have the power (at least conceptually) to change social and political circumstances, but it is another thing to be able to ensure that such a change will occur. Indeed, protest and resistance afford individuals or vulnerable groups the opportunity to voice their concerns and interrogate the status quo, but protest and resistance do not always precipitate change.

Therefore, radical ontology understands that to engage in protest and resistance is a necessary condition but not a sufficient condition to precipitate real change. In other words, we need to engage in protest and resistance to precipitate change (necessary condition), but merely engaging in protest and resistance may not ensure the change we seek (sufficient condition).

Radical freedom entails being realistic that our protest against power structures may get us little mileage, and to resist and complain may, of course, make some ground; yet protest against self-degradation and low self-esteem is indeed the greatest form of resistance. To create oneself in the face of political policies that seem to prolong suffering and displacement is the greatest protest of all. Paul Tillich's helpful work *The Courage to Be* inspires such radical ontology by noting that in face of "threats to being," we anesthetize our spirits so that we may have a more meaningful existence. In applying Sartre's existential notion "the essence of humankind is existence," Tillich writes:

> This sentence is like a flash of light which illuminates the whole Existentialist scene. One could call it the most despairing and the most courageous sentence in all Existentialist literature. What it says is that there is no essential nature of man, except in the one point that he can make of himself what he wants. Man creates what he is. Nothing is given to him to determine his creativity. The essence of his being—the "should-be, the ought-to-be"—is not something which he finds; he makes. Man is what he makes of

> himself. And the courage to be as oneself is the courage to make of
> oneself what one wants to be.[2]

We must go on protesting and practicing radical democracy so that the most vulnerable feels that she has stock in the distribution of resources. West is right that at our very being, human dignity animates the power within, turning whispering complaints to a yell of protest. Yet that same dignity gives a greater power "to create ourselves."

As noted in the previous chapter, Foucault's technology of the self gives radical democracy and individuality existential value in that individuals may be able to carry out this radical creation of themselves. In an essay, "The Ethics of Michel Foucault," James W. Bernauer and Michel Mahon discuss what is entailed in Foucault's technology of self, which is refashioning ourselves as ethical subjects. In their assessment of *The History of Sexuality*, they contend,

> A central enterprise of the second and third volumes in Foucault's
> history of sexuality, then, is to "investigate how individuals were
> led to practice, on themselves and on others, a hermeneutics of
> desire," an investigation of how we have been fashioned and have
> fashioned ourselves as ethical subjects. While ethics is the domain
> of such an analysis, its aim is to provoke and sustain a form of
> resistance to newly recognized political forces.[3]

The best way to resist oppression is to resist the discursive factors undergirding our negative sense of self. Unfortunately, one way to perpetuate oppression is to accept an assigned ontology convincing oppressed people that things are the way they should be.

Therefore, the most helpful way to reconfigure one's ontology, or as Foucault has it, engage in a technology of the self, is by existentially creating a radical ontology. This creation may not completely evade social, cultural, and political constraints. Yet, what is helpful is the realization that any rule or law of discourse negatively affecting well-being is exempted from the ontological creative process. The lesson learned that forms Foucault's later works is that we have a moral responsibility not to abide by the rules of discourse, but to fashion our own existence. I close this chapter by offering the advice of Frantz Fanon who suggests that the more realistic demand is to change ourselves:

2. Tillich, *Courage to Be*, 149–50.

3. Bernauer and Mahon, "Ethics of Michel Foucault," 148.

> Come, then, comrades; it would be as well to decide at once to change our ways. We must shake off the heavy darkness in which we were plunged, and leave it behind. The new day which is already at hand must find us firm, prudent, and resolute.[4]

Fanon reminds us not to plunge ourselves into the existential abyss whereby we allow structure and constraints to give us our ontology, our being. Rather, we stand resolute against the contrary winds of objectification, pejorative truth-claims, and political agendas that do not have our best interests in mind. We are the masters of our fate, and we are discursive agents who determine the conditions for the possibility of our own experience.

Radical Epistemology

The foundation for an ethic of radical freedom relies on Cornel West's notion of radical historicism, which I established is not so radical, until I bring it in a discursive dialogue with Foucault's concept of power and power's relationship with knowledge and truth. Therefore, historicism together with Foucault's overall genealogical methodology will produce a robust epistemological perspective, resulting in a theoretical concept of truth that: empowers not enslaves; heals not hurt; and that precipitates well-being instead of worsening it. This chapter dives deeper into this new epistemology. Let's call it "radical epistemology." Radical epistemology states that truth: (1) always considers context and history; (2) results from power/knowledge relations within a specific context and therefore considers the well-being and flourishing of individuals; (3) is always truth with a lowercase "t," making these claims merely properties of the statements, sentences, and propositions expressing them.

In the case with (1) that notions of truth are not notions at all, but rather claims that individuals within particular communities share generally and consent upon. The value of West's version of radical historicism is affirmation of what local communities and contexts value. The value here is that other communities and contexts cannot assign value to context outside of the particular local context under consideration. As simple as this seems, failure to adhere to this historicist position devalues difference, resulting in racism, marginalization, xenophobia, and other social, cultural, and political maladies. Recall one of the aspects of historicism and pragmatic notions

---

4. Fanon, *Wretched of the Earth*, 311.

of truth is anti-realism. Realism promotes Cartesian concepts that contend that minds accurately mirror the world. In other words, our thoughts accurately represent a certain reality. Anti-realism contests our ability to accurately correlate perceptions of things to the things in the world. Progressive pragmatists like Rorty, Quine, and Sellars are either proponents or allies of anti-realism because of epistemological reasons. One reason is to contest Cartesian commitment to indubitable truths and philosophic foundations. Realism's dogmatic dispositions about objective reality and truth ignore cultural and historical contributions to how people experience reality. Progressive pragmatists see reality and truth as malleable, infallible, and changeable.

Like progressive pragmatism, Cornel West rejects the Cartesian conception of truth as indubitable and infallible, but his pragmatic brand evades Cartesian philosophy for an additional reason. As already noted and perhaps worth restating *The American Evasion of Philosophy*'s subtitle bears some resemblance to the methodologies of Nietzsche and Foucault. West's subtitle, *A Genealogy of Pragmatism*, similar to Nietzsche's *On the Genealogy of Morals* and Foucault's genealogical books, offers an alternative historical perspective to pragmatism, which is, firstly, the inclusion of nonphilosophers to the progressive pragmatist canon. But a second reason, and apropos for a polemic against realism, is the depiction *prophetic*. Prophetic here resembles the social justice of Old Testament prophets like Amos and Micah, and more contemporary advocates like Reinhold Niebuhr and W. E. B. Du Bois. Hence, prophetic pragmatism denies internal conceptions about reality that demean the value of others. Devaluing cultures and races because of aesthetic, religious, and cultural differences, mirrors one's bias, under the guise of objectivity and at the chagrin of those cultures. Protracted anti-Black racism, for example, comes from negative conceptions about Black intelligence and morality from people who believe these conceptions to be absolutely and objectively true. Cornel West is right to reject realism because the posture of the perceiver determines whether or not what they perceive possesses positive or negative attributes. If realism proves true, then negative notions about Black people, for example, confirm what the racist mind perceives.

Radical epistemology believes that conceptions of truth and the grammar of truth are essentially understood as "truth claims," and that there is no such thing as a garden-variety truth claim that is capable of transcending culture and history. This position is inspired by both West's notion of radical historicism and Foucault's denial of "epistemic sovereignty." In the case of the former, radical epistemology states that truth is changeable and historically, contextually and, I might add, existentially situated. This position also entails an outright negation of any notion of either objective or absolute truth. Truth claims are local, which necessarily means that truth claims vary from culture to culture and are only true for that historical moment. This means that a meaningful truth claim for the African American community may not necessarily be meaningful for, say, a Latino American culture and moreover, pervasive truth claims for the African American culture today may not be the case in, say, ten years.

On the other hand, historicism requires reconstruction, because it fails to consider the power/knowledge relations at work, even in a local context. Therefore we must weigh truth claims against individual fulfillment, and reconsider how these claims, universal or local, result from power/knowledge relations. Truth claims must in no way violate individual flourishing and well-being, which essentially means that the individual will not embrace all of the community's claims.

For example, let's suppose a woman in a particular Black church believes she's called to ministry and pastoring. Yet she is a member of a church that embraces the truth claim that God forbids women to serve as pastors. I use the Black church in this example, because of intersectionality indicative of Black women's experiences. As a Black woman who has membership in a church that forbids her to pastor, she has to endure three unfortunate realities: racism, sexism, and ableism. Other than racism, truth claims of her local context preclude well-being and flourishing. Her local context strips her ability to serve as a pastor, because this context sees Paul's directive—"let your women keep silent in the church, for I forbid them to speak"[5]—as a direct command by God. In other words, given that God said it, the truth claim—"it is wrong for women to be preachers"—is absolute for that context. The woman who feels pastoring as a meaningful vocation has the freedom to deny such a truth claim. Radical epistemology argues that a truth claim like this one is entirely relative and the pervasiveness of the truth claim is fanned and fueled by power/knowledge relations existing during a particular moment in history.

Pervasive truth claims within particular communities result from power/knowledge relations, and we accept them only inasmuch as we don't forfeit our freedom to live flourishing lives. To make this point, I partially

5. 1 Cor 14:14.

rely on an essay written by Joseph Rouse entitled "Power/Knowledge." Rouse suggests that Foucault, first, rejects the possibility of epistemic sovereignty to mitigate conflicting truth claims. And second, he argues that Foucault presents an understanding of power as dynamic whereby power is a resource owned by all individuals regardless of social and political status. In the case with (3), I use the notion of Truth with a capital "T" as synonymous with mathematical (and only mathematical) facts. Regarding lowercase "t," all truth claims made outside of mathematical facts are at best truth claims pertaining to a local community. This neither minimizes truth claims with a lowercase "t," nor implies that these claims are better construed as beliefs held only by the local community, thereby giving them little epistemic value.

Compared to Foucault's denial of epistemic sovereignty, radical epistemology resists the politicalization of pervasive truth claims. Such resistance implies that we understand yet eschew theories of truth conceived to be indisputable and indubitable. As Foucault notes, discursive factors involved in pervasive notions of truth essentially come from the many ways the powerful disseminate knowledge. Joseph Rouse, in his essay on Foucault's notion of power/knowledge, refers to this pervasiveness and the dissemination of knowledge as epistemic sovereignty. In *Discipline and Punish*, Foucault discusses how in the eighteenth century crimes committed were committed against the king. *Discipline and Punish* begins with a public execution preceded by corporal punishment, which reestablished the authority and power of the king. Whatever the king decided to be the truth of one's crime was truth indeed. The implication here is that sovereign truth was objective and absolute. This epistemic sovereignty is the impetus for so-called notions of objective truth and is the "king's" way to control and provide political surveillance. Epistemic sovereignty stands above discourse to adjudicate conflicts and resolve disputes from competing truth-claims. Rouse notes,

> Although Foucault does not use the term "epistemic sovereignty," it is not hard to see that there is a close parallel within epistemology to the preoccupation of political reflection with sovereignty as Foucault construes it. . . . Just as a sovereign power stands above and adjudicates conflicts among its subject powers, epistemic sovereignty is the standpoint above disputes among competing truth-claims. Epistemic sovereignty constitutes knowledge as the unified

(or consistently unifiable) network of truths that can be extracted from the circulation of conflicting statements.[6]

As noted above, epistemic sovereignty controls discourse by determining what is both rational and legitimate knowledge. By constituting legitimate knowledge and rational truth claims, epistemic sovereignty and political sovereignty serve as surrogates for both local and universal law. By serving as surrogates to local belief systems, epistemic and political sovereignty determine when truth claims are either legitimate or illegitimate.

> Yet this legitimating does not produce knowledge, in the sense of producing new possibilities for truth. Rather, it allows truth to stand forth by suppressing error and irrationality, that is, those statements that do not conform to method and cohere with the regime it establishes. Foucault has the same dual objection to this conception of epistemic sovereignty as to that of political sovereignty. On the one hand, this conception of knowledge overlooks the micropractices through which particular candidates for knowledge and their objects are produced (this network of micropractices is the parallel in Foucault's later work to what he had earlier called a "discursive formation").[7]

To overcome this politicalization of truth, radical epistemology demands, as Foucault argues, that we "cut off the head of the king." When we cut off the head of the king, we free ourselves from sovereign power over our thoughts, beliefs, and convictions. As Foucault suggested, radical epistemology demands that we "break free of the orientation of political thought toward questions of sovereign power and it's legitimacy."[8] However, such freedom is not easy, and even Foucault laments in *The History of Sexuality*,

> At bottom, despite the difference in epochs and objectives, the representation of power has remained under the spell of monarchy. In political thought and analysis, we still have not cut off the head of the king.[9]

Therefore, radical epistemology embraces a thin version of truth, thereby acknowledging truth with a lowercase "t." Truth with a lowercase "t" is always changeable and always relative to this idea of individual fulfillment.

6. Rouse, "Power/Knowledge," 106.

7. Rouse, "Power/Knowledge," 98.

8. Rouse, "Power/Knowledge," 99.

9. Foucault, *History of Sexuality*, 88.

The contrast is Truth with a capital "T," which refers to mathematical Truths like $1 + 1 = 2$. This view is similar to what David Hume calls the "relations of ideas," which he notes

> are the sciences of Geometry, Algebra, and Arithmetic; and in short, every affirmation, which is either intuitively or demonstratively certain. That the square of the hypotenuse is equal to the square of the two sides, is a proposition, which expresses a relation between these figures. That three times five is equal to the half of thirty, expresses a relation between these numbers. Propositions of this kind are discoverable by the mere operation of thought, without dependence on what is any where existent in the universe. Though there never were a circle or triangle in nature, the truths, demonstrated by EUCLID, would for ever retain their certainty and evidence.[10]

I call this Truth with a capital "T" because it is a truth that is not based on context, experience, or history. Neither does this form of Truth result from power/knowledge relations, and more importantly, this Truth makes no assumptions about people and how people exist or are supposed to exist in the world.

Truth with a lowercase "t" considers notions of truth that are similar to radical historicism and, moreover, notions of truth that understand the power and knowledge relations at work. This view of truth contends that truth has value only in particular circumstances. It is similar to what Hume calls "matters of fact." Matters of fact are different from "relations of ideas" in that the latter comes from experience while the former comes from purely mental operations. Like Hume, I argue that the notion of lowercase "t" is, in a word, arbitrary and could not,

> therefore, be discovered in the cause, and the first invention or conception of it, *a priori*, must be entirely arbitrary. And even after it is suggested, the conjunction of it with the cause must appear equally arbitrary; since there are always many other effects, which, to reason, must seem fully as consistent and natural. In vain, therefore, should we pretend to determine any single event, or infer any cause or effect, without the assistance of observation and experience.[11]

---

10. Hume, *Enquiry Concerning Human Understanding*, 15.

11. Hume, *Enquiry Concerning Human Understanding*, 19.

Indeed, individual experience is the critical arbiter for whether or not a person embraces a specific truth. Individuals determine the commensurability between the local and contextual expressions of truth and their own personal value and fulfillment. When a truth claim potentially precludes fulfillment for the individual, the truth claim is merely a property of the sentence and proposition expressing the truth claim. In the introduction to his *Consequences of Pragmatism*, Rorty echoes this point by stating that when uncapitalized, truth "name[s] properties of sentences, or of actions and situations."[12]

Radical epistemology's thin version of truth is not nihilism in that individual truth complies with the truth claims of the local context. The truth claim fails to have relevance if and only if it denies the individual fulfillment and flourishing. This does not mean that individuals within communities have the liberty to determine truth apart from a local context. Having this constraint precludes individuals from creating absurd truth claims like, "It is right for me to kill innocent people." In most if not all contexts, killing innocent people is wrong and even in those contexts where killing appears to be allowed (such as the Holocaust in Germany), the fact that it denies fulfillment to others (namely Jews) makes it wrong. Similar to the example about the imaginary woman who feels a vocation to ministry and pastoring. She is radically free when she dispenses with truth claims that negatively impact her quality of life. Radical epistemology is radical because it unapologetically says "no" to any and all truth claims that deny, limit, and preclude well-being. Stated at the beginning of this book is that in the game of truth, there are winners and there are losers. And there are. For years, Black people, women, and many other marginalized people endured unimaginable terror and existential misfortune in the name of truth. Even today, these communities, along with others, endure denial of certain inalienable rights. Politicians, contesting rights across a myriad of identities, appeal to an understanding of the objective ideal of heterosexual partnership.

It is important to note here that this book seeks not to provide an apologetic or proof for same-sex relationships or women in ministry, but rather to provide losing players with the rules that guarantee defeat in the game of truth. One rule is how power determines truth and how power controls the proliferation of certain versions of truth. Even when considering the highest court of truth, God, for religious enthusiasts, gives absolute truth. Adding insult to existential and epistemological injury are the statements

12. Rorty, *Consequences of Pragmatism*, xiv.

and propositions in the Bible, presumably God's word, confirming certain harmful truth statements. The fact the biblical narratives themselves have contextual, historical, and linguistic components mean very little in negotiating truth. Remember my friend's statement: "the truth is the truth." To interpret this tautology simply means everything written by biblical writers is God's word and therefore, absolutely true. Therefore, if one believes racist, sexist sentiments writers of the Bible expressed, then one loses in the game of truth and thereby forfeits their freedom.

An ethic of radical freedom is a theoretical concept of profound, practical, and protective proportions, ultimately offering a means of transcendence. And in this chapter, a tenet of this transcendence is radical epistemology. We cannot change the minds and hearts of people who have power and influence over our thoughts. But we have absolute control in transcending notions of truth that harm our well-being. With transcendence, losing in the game of truth is tentative and doesn't have to come at an existential lost. Radical freedom entails a radical decision to understand the conditions of truth claims your community embraces. Know the history, the context, and the forces of power energizing truth claims or beliefs. The adage "knowledge is power" posses a paradoxical advantage in two ways. It exposes the knowledge of power while also inspiring us to seek the power of knowledge. Radical epistemology, a foundation of one's personal ethic, occasions existential transcendence where your truth will set you free.

It is truly an insult on integrity to write a book on radical freedom and yet ignore the exemplars of that freedom. A postmodern ethic of radical freedom is more practical than theoretical, or better said, it is theoretical because it is practical. Theory comes from somewhere, and that place is neither libraries nor classrooms where erudite exchanges elucidate and espouse ideas. Rather, the womb that births theory finds fertilization in practice and praxis. No theory emerges without a story. In fact, the theories I discussed here exist because of stories. West's theories of radical historicism and improvisational metaphysics come from experiences as an African American who knows and experiences anti-Black racism in America. I end this book acknowledging feminist and womanist postures who are exemplars of radical freedom. Their stories of transcendence epitomize radical ontology and radical epistemology. Two womanist theorists come to mind: womanist theologian Monica Coleman, and womanist social theorist Patricia Hill Collins. I begin with a brief discussion of Coleman.

Monica Coleman: Womanist Process
Theology and Radical Freedom

Process womanist theologian Monica Coleman has certainly left her mark on theological discourse by being the first process womanist theologian. Her book *Making a Way Out of No Way* carves out new space in theology. Her vision of God and other systematic theological components facilitates transcendence through the terrain of conventional notions of God, Christ, and community. As with a postmodern ethic of radical freedom, Coleman situates her theological conversation as postmodern. As foundational, she begins with Alfred North Whitehead's process metaphysics and then brings into dialogue more recent womanist theologians to provide her framework. Additionally, she advocates for community and commune with African ancestral voices to complement a relational metaphysics. Creative transformation and healing are the indicators of radical freedom.

She opens her text reminding us that theology is personal and practical, which is to say, that practice is theory's antecedent. It's personal as expected. Her professional and academic pilgrimage culminates with womanist process theology, but it's a journey with existential stops along the way. This pilgrimage entails professional and academic eclecticism, comprising of ordination in the African American Methodist Church and scholarly contributions to a variety of disciplines, with her latest book discussing mental health and theology. Though punctuated by Promethean creativity, her theoretical construction of process womanism follows a practical experience peppered by sexual violence.

Before completing graduate work at Claremont, Coleman writes *The Dinah Project: A Handbook for Congregational Responses to Sexual Violence*. Inspiration for this book is Coleman's personal experience and trauma of rape by a fellow male clergyperson. After this trauma, Coleman consulted pastor after pastor until finding one sympathetic enough to provide a ministry of presence. The moment of symbolic transcendence came when she decided to memorialize her experience. She says:

> I decided to create my own ritual. I decided that I wanted to invite friends and family and have a small church ceremony. Maybe the laying on of hands? Something that involved people I loved, a church tradition, and touching.[13]

---

13. Coleman, *Dinah Project*, xi.

This spark of transcendence let off a flame of freedom. In 1997 she facilitated a worship service and called it the Dinah Project. This flame continued, as she admitted the Dinah Project "had taken on a life bigger than me and bigger than the church in which it was founded."[14] For example, Monica Coleman makes this point in *Making a Way Out of No Way*. Years later, a seminary professor and systematic theologian, she restates my position about theory and practice:

> "Theology is autobiography." This phrase is often invoked to illustrate that our constructive theological proposals are intensely personal. They are shaped by our personal histories, our past and current contexts, the specific issues that concern us. They are shaped by whom and what we have encountered—what we read, whom we know, those whom we engage in conversation . . . theology, while personal, cannot be private. It must be something that could apply to someone other than the theologian. It should be something you would recommend to others. It should be something you'd be willing to preach.[15]

The more I reflect on these wise words provided by my friend and fellow Claremont doctoral alumnus, the more I commit to the belief that practical narratives precipitate theoretical formation.

Coleman's insight to philosophy and theology is integrative in that one's personal experiences, whether great or grotesque, inform how one theorizes. In being integrative, theological and philosophical commitments are not products of a disembodied thinker who manages to distance herself from the theories she articulates. Rather, theory emerges from the ruin of marginalization, sexual violence, and depression. Radical freedom then contains moments when such freedom seemed unattainable. Conventional notions of God provide little, if any, meaning amidst the ugliness of rape, violence, and slavery. Even Black liberation theology fails to adjudicate divine absence in the face of undeserved suffering. The construction of a healthier theological paradigm provides the answers implied in the human situation. Process womanist theology provides answers and surfaces as a quintessential antidote for radical freedom. Because through the process (no pun intended) of giving it birth, Coleman learns how to transcend the trauma of violence and victimization by negating notions of truth and

---

14. Coleman, *Dinah Project*, xii.
15. Coleman, *Making a Way*, ix.

reality that limit freedom. As her book suggests, process womanist theology facilitates "a way out of no way."

Patricia Hill Collins: Womanist Epistemology and Radical Freedom

Patricia Hill Collins recasts white male Eurocentric philosophical perspective on truth and knowledge with what she appropriately titles, Black feminist epistemology. As we have seen, with the game of truth, there are winners and losers. Collins is aware of the perils of playing the game from the rules Eurocentrism establishes, yet while playing the same game, Collins invokes different rules. These new rules involve making Black women's subjectivity as foundational, and places shades on normative gazes that belittle these women's value. Black feminist epistemology exalts, includes, and give credibility to the everyday experiences and knowledge produced and shared by Black women across the diaspora. For Collins these experiences include *the use of dialogue in accessing knowledge claims*, an ethic of caring, and an ethic of personal accountability.

The use of dialogue highlights the importance of reciprocity in expressing shared experience and an outright jettison of subject/object relationship. Which is to say that Black women have agency in how they see themselves regardless of how others see them. The normative gaze is an established and accepted gaze but nothing god-given or universally true. Radical freedom gives an adamant "no" to any perception or conception that demeans instead of affirms. But this freedom happens in community and in dialogue in that Black women collectively affirm their worth and value. Through shared experiences, they empower and encourage. Black feminist epistemology values community and communal sharing, for this reason; which means that Black women gain knowledge through dialogue with other women. Regardless of educational background, professional pedigree, or economic disposition, reciprocal sharing precipitates flourishing and well-being. In her own words she lauds the intellectual acumen of all Black women, and asserts their acumen regardless of academic accomplishments:

> Black women intellectuals are neither all academics nor found
> primarily in the Black middle class. Instead, all US Black women
> who somehow contribute to Black feminist thought as critical social theory are deemed to be "intellectuals." They may be

> highly educated. Many are not. For example, nineteenth-century Black feminist activist Sojourner Truth is not typically seen as an intellectual.[16]

Sharing, as Sojourner Truth often did, empowered Black women, while also enlightening others of the strength and value of all women.

An ethic of caring shows that knowledge and truth entail emotion and compassion, which although not entirely cerebral, contribute to depth of knowledge. The nurturing of wisdom depends on emotional intelligence. Collins and others debunk notions of a linear rationality championed by modern male philosophers. Instead, Black feminist epistemology proposes a relational form of rationality. Like Coleman, Collins values the African spirit of community where rationality does not limit itself to an apparatus of logical analysis.[17]

And finally, Collins encourages accountability in that Black women must be accountable while also holding others accountable. No longer will Black women acquiesce to the ideals promulgated by voices of domination and oppression. They must speak truth to power in a myriad of contexts to include political, racial, cultural, and even personal. Though Black women exist within a dominated society that disadvantages them economically, politically, and culturally, they are accountable to each other and their community to fight the good fight. This good fight entails a counter-hegemonic response by writing, lecturing, discussing, and employing other means of creative protest.

A radical posture of selfhood and positive affirmation set the stage for radical epistemology. Transcendence is central in that a Black feminist epistemology considers only the theoretical and practical resources that add value to their lives. Freedom comes from denial and resistance to any theory or implicit notions that devalue them. Recall the Church of Christ context where women accept versions of truth that explicitly deny them access to power.

Black feminist—or shall we say, radical womanist—epistemology exposes Eurocentric-based epistemology that either ignores struggles and experiences of Black women, or implicitly demeans their worth. Thanks to Collins, Coleman, and others, their radical freedom says "no" to notions of truth and knowledge that causes trauma, terror, and trouble.

16. Collins, *Black Feminist Thought*, 17.

17. Collins, *Black Feminist Thought*, 17.

Conclusion

I cannot end a book about radical freedom without recalling the most amazing example that epitomizes strength of character and will, and that is the example of Patricia Ann Wesley. All of the cultural, political, and societal constraints discussed here depict her long life narrative of reaching radical freedom. The youngest of three girls born to Ananias and Nina Russell, her trauma commenced at six years old. Nina Russell died unexpectedly, and her father married perhaps the worst nightmare of stepmothers. All of the things you never want young Black girls to hear bombarded her consciousness like "a rushing mighty wind." She was pregnant at sixteen by a young lad who initially denied his fatherhood, and when he finally came around, he died two years later. She then married into a relationship where everything that could go wrong did. Domestic violence from her husband, neglect from in-laws, sexism, racism, and psychological damage of gigantic proportions were ingredients in her narrative. Yet despite constraints, and without reading Sartre, West, or Foucault, she said "no" to the epistemological incarceration of her church by leaving it. She worked three jobs, and insisted her children attend college. And she maintained self-worth regardless of context and conditions for possibilities of failure saying otherwise. She is the embodiment of transcendence and the epitome of radical freedom.

Bibliography

Amesbury, Richard. *Morality and Social Criticism: The Force of Reasons in Discursive Practice*. New York: Palgrave Macmillan, 2005.

Anderson, Victor. *Beyond Ontological Blackness: An Essay on African American Religious and Cultural Criticism*. New York: Continuum, 1995.

———. "Is Cornel West also Among the Theologians? The Shadow of the Divine in the Religious Thought of Cornel West." In *Cornel West: A Critical Reader*, edited by George Yancy, 139–53. Malden, MA: Blackwell, 2001.

Aristotle. *Nicomachean Ethics*. Translated by Martin Ostwald. Upper Saddle River, NJ: Prentice Hall, 1999.

Artaud, Antonin. *To Have Done with the Judgment of God*. Radio broadcast, KPFA, October 15, 1968.

Ayer, Alfred Jules. *Language, Truth, and Logic*. New York: Dover, 1936.

Belsey, Catherine. *Poststructuralism: A Very Short Introduction*. Oxford: Oxford University Press, 2002.

Berkeley, George. *George Berkeley: Three Dialogues Between Hylas and Philonous*, reprinted. Chicago: Open Court, 1906.

Bernauer, James W., and Michel Mahon. "The Ethics of Michel Foucault." In *The Cambridge Companion to Foucault*, edited by Gary Gutting, 141–58. Cambridge: Cambridge University Press, 1994.

Best, Steven, and Douglas Kellner. *Postmodern Theory: Critical Interrogations*. New York: Guilford, 2008.

Bouveresse, Jacques. "Why I Am So Very UnFrench." In *Philosophy in France Today*, edited by Alan Montefiore, 9–33. Cambridge: Cambridge University Press, 1983.

Carnap, Rudolf. *Logical Construction of the World and Pseudoproblems in Philosophy*. Peru, IL: Open Court, 2003.

Church, Alonzo. "Intensional Semantics." In *The Philosophy of Language*, edited by A. P. Martinich, 77–84. 2nd ed. Oxford: Oxford University Press, 1990.

Coleman, Monica. *The Dinah Project: A Handbook for Congregational Response to Sexual Violence*. Eugene, OR: Wipf & Stock, 2004.

———. *Making a Way Out of No Way*. Minneapolis: Fortress, 2008.

Collins, Patricia Hill. *Black Feminist Thought: Knowledge, Consciousness, and the Politics of Empowerment*. 2nd ed. London: Routledge Taylor & Francis, 2014.

Copeland, M. Shawn. "Cornel West's Improvisational Philosophy of Religion." In *Cornel West: A Critical Reader*, edited by George Yancey, 154–66. Malden, MA: Blackwell, 2001.

Cowan, Rosemary. *Cornel West: The Politics of Redemption*. Cambridge: Polity, 2003.

Crisp, Roger. "Ethics." In *Routledge Encyclopedia of Philosophy*, edited by E. Craig. London: Routledge, 1998. http://www.rep.routledge.com/article/L132.

Cunningham, Michael. *The Hours*. London: Picador, 2000.

Danto, Arthur. "Analytic Philosophy." *Social Research* 47.4 (Winter 1980) 615–16.

Davidson, Donald. *Inquiries into Truth and Interpretation*. Oxford: Oxford University Press, 1984.

Descartes, Rene. *The Philosophical Writings of Descartes*. Vol. 1. Translated by John Cottinghan, Robert Stoothoff, and Dugald Murdoch. Cambridge: Cambridge University Press, 1985.

Dewey, John. "Creative Democracy: The Task Before Us." In *John Dewey: The Later Works, 1925–1953*, edited by Jo Ann Boydston and Anne Sharpe, 224–30. Vol. 14, 1939–1941. Carbondale: Southern Illinois University Press, 1988.

———. *Democracy and Education*. The Middle Works 9, 1916. Edited by Jo Ann Boydston. Carbondale: Southern Illinois University Press, 1980.

———. *Experience and Nature*. New York: W. W. Norton, 1929.

———. "Half-Hearted Naturalism." *Journal of Philosophy* 24 (February 3, 1927) 59–73.

———. "My Pedagogic Creed." In *The Early Works of John Dewey, 1882–1898*, edited by J. A. Boydston. Vol. 5, *1895–1898*.

Dreyfus, Hubert L., and Paul Rabinow. *Michel Foucault: Beyond Structuralism and Hermeneutics*. 2nd ed. Chicago: University of Chicago Press, 1983. Carbondale: Southern Illinois University Press, 1975.

Dummett, Michael. *Truth and Other Enigmas*. Cambridge: Harvard University Press, 1978.

Dyson, Michael Eric. "The Ghost of Cornel West: What Happened to America's Most Exciting Black Scholar?" *The New Republic*, April 19, 2015. https://newrepublic.com/article/121550/cornel-wests-rise-fall-our-most-exciting-black-scholar-ghost.

Fanon, Frantz. *The Wretched of the Earth*. Translated by Constance Farrington. New York: Grove, 1963.

Foucault, Michel. *The Archaeology of Knowledge*. New York: Pantheon, 1972.

———. *The Birth of the Clinic: An Archaeology of Medical Perception*. New York: Vintage, 1994.

———. "The Confession of the Flesh." In *Power/Knowledge: Selected Interviews and Other Writings, 1972–1977*, by Michel Foucault, edited by Colin Gordon, 194–228. New York: Pantheon, 1980.

———. *Discipline and Punish: The Birth of the Prison*. New York: Vintage, 1995.

———. "The Discourse on Language." In *The Archaeology of Knowledge*, translated by Rupert Swyer, 215–38. New York: Pantheon, 1972.

———. *The History of Sexuality*. 3 vols. Translated by Robert Hurley. New York: Vintage, 1988–90.

———. *The History of Sexuality*. Vol. 2, *The Use of Pleasure*. Translated by Robert Hurley. New York: Vintage, 1990.

———. *Language, Counter-Memory, Practice: Selected Essays and Interviews*. Edited by D. F. Bouchard. Ithaca, NY: Cornell University Press, 1977.

————. *Madness and Civilization: A History of Insanity in the Age of Reason*. New York: Vintage, 1973.

————. "Nietzsche, Genealogy, History." In *Language, Counter-Memory, Practice: Selected Essays and Interviews by Michel Foucault*, edited by D. F. Bouchard, 139–64. Ithaca, NY: Cornell University Press, 1977.

————. *The Order of Things: An Archaeology of the Human Sciences*. New York: Pantheon, 1971.

————. "Par dela le bien et le mal." *Actuel* 14 (November 1971) 42.

————. *Society Must Be Defended: Lectures at the Collège de France 1975–76*. Compiled under the direction of Mauro Bertani, Alessandro Fontana, and François Ewald. Translated by David Macey. New York: Picador, 2003.

Friedrich, Otto. "France's Philosopher of Power." *Time*, November 16, 1981.

Godfrey-Smith, Peter. "Dewey and the Question of Realism." *Nous* 50 (March 2016) 73–89.

————. "Dewey on Naturalism, Realism, and Science." *Philosophy of Science* 69 (September 2002) 25–35.

Goodman, Nelson. *Ways of Worldmaking*. Indianapolis: Hackett, 1978.

Gordon, Colin. *Power/Knowledge: Selected Interviews and Other Writings 1972–1977 by Michel Foucault*. Translated by Colin Gordon et al. New York: Pantheon, 1980.

Gordon, Lewis R. "The Unacknowledged Fourth Tradition: An Essay on Nihilism, Decadence, and the Black Intellectual Tradition in the Existential Pragmatic Thought of Cornel West." In *Cornel West: A Critical Reader*, edited by George Yancy, 38–58. Malden, MA: Blackwell, 2001.

Gross, Neil. *Richard Rorty: The Making of an American Philosopher*. Chicago: University of Chicago Press, 2008.

Gutting, Gary, ed. *The Cambridge Companion to Foucault*. Cambridge: Cambridge University Press, 1994.

————. *Foucault: A Very Short Introduction*. Oxford: Oxford University Press, 2005.

Hayman, Ronald. *Nietzsche: The Great Philosophers*. New York: Routledge, 1999.

Headley, Clevis. "Cornel West on Prophesy, Pragmatism, and Philosophy: A Critical Evaluation of Prophetic Pragmatism." In *Cornel West: A Critical Reader*, edited by George Yancy, 59–82. Malden, MA: Blackwell, 2001.

hooks, bell. "Postmodern Blackness." *Postmodern Culture* 1.1 (September 1990).

————. *Yearning: Race, Gender, and Cultural Politics*. Boston: South End, 1990.

Horrocks, Chris, and Zoran Jevtic. *Introducing Foucault*. London: Icon, 2007.

Hume, David. *An Enquiry Concerning Human Understanding: A Letter from a Gentleman to His Friend in Edinburgh*. Edited by Eric Steinberg. Indianapolis: Hackett, 1977. Originally published in *English Philosophers of the Seventeenth and Eighteenth Centuries*, New York: P. F. Collier & Son, 1910.

Johnson, Clarence Sholé. *Cornel West and Philosophy: The Quest for Social Justice*. London: Routledge, 2003.

Kant, Immanuel. *Critique of Pure Reason*. Translated by H. J. Paton. New York: Penguin, 1981.

————. *Groundwork of the Metaphysics of Morals*. Translated by H. J. Paton. New York: Harper & Row, 1964.

————. *Prolegomena to Any Future Metaphysics*. Translated by Lewis White Beck. New York: Macmillan, 1956.

Lemos, Noah. "Epistemology and Ethics." In *The Oxford Handbook of Epistemology*, edited by Paul Moser, 479–512. Oxford: Oxford University Press, 2002.

McGinn, Colin. "Radical Interpretation and Epistemology." In *Truth and Interpretation: Perspective on the Philosophy of Donald Davidson*, edited by Ernest LePore. Oxford: Basil Blackwell, 1986.

McHoul, Alec, and Wendy Grace. *A Foucault Primer: Discourse, Power and the Subject*. New York: New York University Press, 1993.

Mendieta, Eduardo. "'What It Means to Be Human!': A Conversation with Cornel West." *Critical Philosophy of Race* 5.2 (2017) 137–70.

Miller, James. *The Passion of Michel Foucault*. Cambridge: Harvard University Press, 1993.

Nidditch, Peter H., ed. *John Locke: An Essay Concerning Human Understanding*. Oxford: Oxford University Press, 1975.

Niebuhr, Reinhold. *Children of Light and Children of Darkness: A Vindication of Democracy and a Critique of its Traditional Defense*. New York: Scribner, 1945.

Pittman, John P. "'Radical Historicism,' Antiphilosophy, and Marxism." In *Cornel West: A Critical Reader*, edited by George Yancy, 224–44. Malden, MA: Blackwell, 2001.

Putnam, Hilary W. "Pragmatism Resurgent: A Reading of *The American Evasion of Philosophy*." In *Cornel West: A Critical Reader*, edited by George Yancy, 19–37. Malden, MA: Blackwell, 2001.

———. "A Reconsideration of Deweyan Democracy." In *Renewing Philosophy*, by Hilary Putnam, 187–200. Cambridge: Harvard University Press, 1992.

Putnam, Hilary W., and Ruth Anna Putnam. "Education for Democracy." In *Hilary Putnam: Words and Life*, edited by James Conant, 221–42. Cambridge: Harvard University Press, 1995.

Quine, Willard Van Orman. *From a Logical Point of View*. Cambridge: Harvard University Press, 1963. Noted in Richard Rorty, *Philosophy and the Mirror of Nature*. Princeton: Princeton University Press, 1980.

———. *Word and Object*. Cambridge: MIT Press, 1960.

Rorty, Richard. "Cartesian Epistemology and Changes in Ontology." In *Contemporary American Philosophy*, edited by John E. Smith, 273–92. 2nd series. New York: Yale University Press, 1970.

———. *Consequences of Pragmatism: Essays, 1972–1980*. Minneapolis: University of Minnesota Press, 1982.

———. *Contingency, Irony, and Solidarity*. Cambridge: Cambridge University Press, 1989.

———. *Essays on Heidegger and Others: Philosophical Papers*. Vol. 2. Cambridge: Cambridge University Press, 1991.

———. *The Linguistic Turn: Recent Essays in Philosophical Method*. Chicago: University of Chicago Press, 1967.

———. *Objectivity, Relativism, and Truth: Philosophical Papers*. Vol. 1. Cambridge: Cambridge University Press, 1991.

———. *Philosophy and Social Hope*. New York: Penguin, 1999.

———. *Philosophy and the Mirror of Nature*. Princeton: Princeton University Press, 1979.

———. *Truth and Progress: Philosophical Papers*. Vol. 3. Cambridge: Cambridge University Press, 1998.

Rouse, Joseph. "Power/Knowledge." In *The Cambridge Companion to Foucault*, edited by Gary Gutting, 92–114. Cambridge: Cambridge University Press, 1994.

Searle, John R. "Proper Names and Intentionality." In *The Philosophy of Language*, edited by A. P. Martinich, 326–42. 2nd ed. Oxford: Oxford University Press, 1990.

Sellars, Willard. "Empiricism and the Philosophy of Mind." In *Minnesota Studies in the Philosophy of Science*, edited by Herbert Feigl and Michael Scriven. Vol. 1. Minneapolis: University of Minnesota Press, 1956.

Taylor, Astra, dir. *Examined Life: Philosophy Is in the Streets*. New York: Zeitgeist Films, 2009.

Tillich, Paul. *The Courage to Be*. New Haven: Yale University Press, 2000.

———. "Relation of Metaphysics and Theology." *The Review of Metaphysics* 1 (September 1956) 57–58.

———. *Systematic Theology*. Vol. 1. Chicago: University of Chicago Press, 1951.

Visker, Rudi. *Michel Foucault: Genealogy as Critique*. Translated by Chris Turner. London: Verso, 1995.

Weaver, William G. "Richard Rorty and the Radical Left." *Virginia Law Review* 78 (1992) 729–57.

West, Cornel. *The American Evasion of Philosophy: A Genealogy of Pragmatism*. Madison: University of Wisconsin Press, 1989.

———. *The Cornel West Reader*. New York: Basic Civitas, 1999.

———. *Democracy Matters: Winning the Fight Against Imperialism*. New York: Penguin, 2004.

———. *The Ethical Dimensions of Marxist Thought*. New York: Monthly Review, 1991.

———. "Ethics, Historicism, and The Marxist Tradition." PhD dissertation, Princeton University, 1980.

———. "A Genealogy of Modern Racism." In *Prophecy Deliverance: An Afro-American Revolutionary Christianity*, by Cornel West, 47–68. Grand Rapids: Eerdmans, 1988.

———. "Nietzsche's Prefiguration of Postmodern American Philosophy." In *Early Postmodernism: Foundational Essays*, edited by Paul A. Bové et al., 265–89. Durham, NC: Duke University Press, 1995. Reprinted in *The Cornel West Reader*, New York: Basic Civitas, 1999.

———. "A Philosophical View of Easter." In *The Cornel West Reader*, edited by George Yancy, 415–20. New York: Basic Civitas, 1999. Published earlier in *Dialogue: A Journal of Theology* 19.1 (Winter 1980) 21–24; and in *Prophetic Fragments: Illuminations of the Crises in American Religion and Culture*, 260–66. Grand Rapids: Eerdmans, 1993.

———. *Prophesy Deliverance: An Afro-American Revolutionary Christianity*. Philadelphia: Westminster, 1982.

———. *Prophetic Fragments: Illuminations of the Crises in American Religion and Culture*. Grand Rapids: Eerdmans, 1988.

———. *Sketches of My Culture*. Music CD, Artimis Records, B00005OC67, 2001.

West, Cornel, with David Ritz. *Brother West: Living and Loving Out Loud, A Memoir*. New York: Smiley, 2009.

West, Cornel, and John Rajchman. *Post-Analytic Philosophy*. New York: Columbia University Press, 1985.

Wolterstorff, Nicholas. *Reason within the Bounds of Religion*. Grand Rapids: Eerdmans, 1984.

Wood, Mark David. *Cornel West and the Politics of Prophetic Pragmatism*. Chicago: University of Illinois Press, 2000.

Yancy, George, ed. *Cornel West: A Critical Reader*. Malden, MA: Blackwell, 2001.